SUE CLEAVER is an actress bes[illegible] Grimshaw in the long-running ITV soap *Coronation Street*. Her other TV credits include: *City Central*; *Dinnerladies*; *This is Personal: The Hunt for the Yorkshire Ripper*; *Peak Practice; Casualty; Reckless: The Sequel*; *The Cops*; *King Girl*; *Band of Gold* and *A Touch of Frost*. She took part in *I'm a Celebrity: Get Me Out of Here!* in 2022, and is a regular panellist on *Loose Women*. This is Sue's first book, and she wants to make it count.

# Sue Cleaver

# A Work in Progress

B L O O M S B U R Y   P U B L I S H I N G
LONDON • OXFORD • NEW YORK • NEW DELHI • SYDNEY

BLOOMSBURY PUBLISHING
Bloomsbury Publishing Plc
50 Bedford Square, London, WC1B 3DP, UK
Bloomsbury Publishing Ireland Limited,
29 Earlsfort Terrace, Dublin 2, D02 AY28, Ireland

BLOOMSBURY, BLOOMSBURY PUBLISHING and the Diana logo are trademarks of Bloomsbury Publishing Plc

First published in Great Britain 2024
This edition published 2025



A catalogue record for this book is available from the British Library

ISBN: HB: 978-1-5266-7870-6; PB: 978-1-5266-8130-0;
eBook: 978-1-5266-8129-4; ePDF: 978-1-5266-8128-7

2 4 6 8 10 9 7 5 3 1

Typeset by Newgen KnowledgeWorks Pvt. Ltd., Chennai, India
Printed and bound in Great Britain by CPI Group (UK) Ltd, Croydon CR0 4YY

FSC www.fsc.org MIX Paper | Supporting responsible forestry FSC® C171272

To find out more about our authors and books visit www.bloomsbury.com and sign up for our newsletters
For product safety related questions contact productsafety@bloomsbury.com

To my two mothers. Freda for your boundless love and guidance, and Lesley for your courageous heart and the gift of love.

My deepest gratitude and love.

# CONTENTS

# PROLOGUE

> 'As you get older, people start saying, "Oh yeah, you should retire. You should do this. You should..." No, guys. Do not tell me what to do. I should be in control of what I am capable of. Ladies, don't let anybody tell you you are ever past your prime. Never give up.'
>
> Michelle Yeoh

To say that sixty-year-old Michelle Yeoh was speaking my language as she collected her 2023 Oscar is something of an understatement. While her acceptance speech might have been focused on the film industry, the ageism and sexism she referred to remains rife in so many other areas of life, which is something most of us midlife women know only too well. So I loved what she said on that stage, clutching the highest honour an actor could achieve – and way past the idea of a woman's prime. As if!

I've always been struck by the way women are viewed once they reach a certain age and, now I'm there myself, all the more so. I don't want to be silent in the conversations that determine the rest of my life. And I don't think other women should be either.

Landmark birthdays are often a time for taking stock, for looking at what's gone before and examining our hopes and dreams for the future, for learning from the past and taking those lessons forward into what we do next. And for me, turning sixty has certainly been a case in point.

I've spent many, many years not really knowing who I am and reaching out for solutions in all the wrong places. I've spent a lifetime feeling that I don't belong and looking to find that sense of being a part of something in ways that have ended up with me being pretty hard on myself – and on my family. I found that self-destruct button and I pressed it again and again and again, in part because I had no idea how to express the way I was feeling.

It hasn't always been easy and there's been plenty of getting it wrong, though I hope that learning from my mistakes has helped me to grow as a person and begin to find the answers I have always so desperately sought. It's only now, at last, that I'm beginning to find my true voice – and that makes me want to use it. I certainly haven't got to this point only to be ignored or patronised, to be disregarded on the basis of my age or anything else, especially given I'm finally starting to understand who I really am and what makes me tick after some very tough times along the way.

I'll be honest, my role in *Coronation Street* is not the only one I have found myself playing, week in, week out. As women we often find ourselves expected to be all things to all people. We are pulled in so many different directions and I want to use the prism of my own experience to explore this – and how society sees us as we age – through snapshots of my life. In this book I will share my journey so far – warts and all – and through that hopefully encourage other women who've found they've somehow lost the essence of themselves – and it really is all too easy to lose sight of who we are and what we need to thrive.

This is a book of two halves, the first looking at the things in my life that led me to reach a place where I knew things really had to change, and the second revealing the insights and wisdom that have made me the happier, more confident woman I have now become. Call it a manifesto for midlife, if you will.

*A Work in Progress* is a book for women, looking at shared female experience and learnings from the good times and the not-so-good, and how the episodes in my own life have helped shape the person I am today. It's about learning to be kinder to ourselves, to forgive ourselves (because which of us hasn't beaten ourselves up about this, that and the other over the years – even when it's about things that are absolutely no fault of our own?). It's about being able to look at the years ahead with excitement and positivity rather than dread.

It's about working out where our demons, insecurities and belief systems come from and asking questions about ourselves so that we can gain self-knowledge, become more accepting of who we are, and find happiness and inner peace. It will look at the events in my life that have made me, well, me – from the early insecurities of my childhood and my adoption, from life on *The Street* to a reality TV show that pushed me to my limits. I will talk about how I learned that shouting the loudest doesn't always mean being right or winning an argument. I'll also share details of my battle with the booze, how I coped with menopause, taught my son to be a hugger and why I find it impossible to conform.

And, finally, it's a book about not allowing life to consume us, about stopping the self-doubt creeping in and taking over – something that seems to happen to so many of us as we get older; we have been silenced and we're still being silenced, but it's never been more important to make our voices heard – and it's never too late to do this. We do not want to be invisible; we need to be seen. And understood. And be supported by each other and the men in our lives.

I want women to understand that they're okay – *we're* okay – despite the fact we get such a bloody hard time. It shouldn't be this way, but we're all right as we are and we don't need to be pigeonholed, patronised or put out to pasture (thank you).

There's a lot of chat about older women's rage, but this is absolutely not a rage book – although I will share the frustrations at the way that we are sometimes dismissed and diminished. I prefer to think of it as a call to arms to unite us against the easy and lazy stereotyping of women, young, old or otherwise – but particularly older women. And I'm not just thinking of mother-in-law jokes or nan jokes. Women are regularly stereotyped, even in novels and on screen (if the parts are there for us in the first place), so I want to look at how we can change this. After all, even (!) in midlife, we still have so much to offer the world – and we need to remember our value. Oh, and let's agree on something here; that value is not solely linked to our age or fertility.

Is it?

You'd like to think not, but so often we face comments or situations which make us question whether this is really the case. It often feels like no one seems to value our years of experience; that they're saying because we might have lost that lustre of youth, we are no longer deemed worthy enough to be useful. In short, we are made to feel that we're way past our sell-by date, which is why I found what Michelle Yeoh said so inspiring.

In fact, as I approached my sixtieth birthday, I appeared on a podcast where the host jokingly said to me, 'That's it now. You're at the top of the rollercoaster and you're about to take the plunge to the bottom.'

I was somewhat taken aback. As far as I was concerned, I was on the way up, not down! But then, this is how so many people seem to see us *older* women. It's almost as though we're being told that we've done our bit and we're no longer relevant, so could we please just shuffle off quietly and not make a fuss. So much for it being the twenty-first century.

Let's not shuffle off, ladies, and let's get a few things straight:

- We are not merely shadows of our former selves. Hey, we might even be improved versions, the best we've ever been.
- We can't just be dismissed.
- We cannot be silenced.
- We have things to say, and they matter.

So at what point do we start believing the rhetoric telling us what we say and what we do *doesn't* count? That's what I'll be exploring, as well as how to turn the tide on the self-doubt and lack of confidence which has plagued me for so much of my own life – as you'll see in the stories I share.

Progress is being made, and I am delighted to see so many younger women finding and using their voices, passionately advocating for themselves to make change. It makes me hugely positive for the generations to come. But what about us, the middle-aged and the older women, who society has largely conditioned to accept their lot and not make waves? We still have so much to give and enjoy… so what next?

*This* is next: we start a new conversation – and that's exactly why I have been so excited to write this book. I've spent a lifetime worrying about what people might think or what impact my words might have on someone else, so it never felt like the right time to talk about myself or my private life – at least until now. Coming to peace, or the most peaceful I have been with myself, quite late in life is a joy I want other women to feel.

How have I moved forward? It's been through learning more about how I work. About looking inside rather than outside for answers. You don't need an expert, or to be an expert yourself – you just need to change the way you look at things, because the long and the short of it is, you cannot solve a problem with the same thinking that created it in the first place. You need a new way.

It is not always easy to create the mental space to make the necessary change. We have so much going on in our lives that often the quiet moments can be blocked out by all the other shit. But we have to listen for them, do what we can to quieten the noise, and trust ourselves that we will get that little bit of wisdom, that little bit of insight. It really can make an enormous difference, though I admit I haven't fully perfected the art of putting it into practice on every single occasion. As the title of this book suggests, I'm still very much a work in progress.

Because of my work, or the interviews I have (very rarely) done, I have had so many women reaching out to me over the years. I realise, of course, that my own experience as a sixty-something woman may have some unique elements – like being on the telly – but so much more is shared. And this is the stuff we need to start talking about, whether it's about putting everyone else's needs first and ignoring our own or keeping our feelings bottled up because we feel we have no choice, or whether it's about navigating relationships or dealing with grief. All of these things are universal and all of them impact who we become and how we live our lives in midlife and beyond.

It is never too late to learn to prioritise ourselves and to move forward to a better, brighter future, and when better to start than right now?

It's our time, ladies. Let's bloody grasp it with both hands.

# Part One

# THE THINGS THAT HAVE MADE ME… ME

# 1

# Who Are You?

To make effective changes in our lives, we are often told that we need to take stock of what's gone before, to look at the things that have made us who we are. But when I finally reached a point where I knew things needed to be different and I couldn't go on as I was, the process of looking back was something that I found very difficult to do. There were many periods of my life that were painful to revisit in forensic detail – but, equally, I believed that to move forward, understanding the past would need to be a huge part of the process. Was I right about that? Let's say the answer has been one of many revelations on my journey so far.

It's all too common for middle-aged and older women to lose their sense of self, but what happens if you never really had that in the first place? Whatever our background or circumstances, I think most of us go through periods where we struggle with our identities or question things about ourselves. I was certainly an expert in the field, but for me it started very early, because I was adopted as a newborn baby. I was aware of this even as a very young child. In fact, I don't remember a time when I wasn't, which, perhaps, was fairly unusual back then. Certainly, every time we went to the GP, he would ask whether I could just step outside for a moment while he spoke to my mother. I would tell him there was no need, that I knew I was adopted, and as such my mother wouldn't be able to tell him whether whatever condition he wanted to know about ran in my family, because we had no idea.

Despite the fact that I was never made to feel lesser in any way by my loving family, not knowing who I was or where I came from added another layer of uncertainty about myself, which has underlined my life for as long as I can remember, until relatively recently.

In many ways, I had a wonderful childhood, but like a lot of adoptees, knowing that I was different from the rest of my family was difficult. As a child that difference really mattered to me. It's not that you'd have looked at my parents and me and thought, *Well, she stands out like a sore thumb*. In fact, people used to say I looked like my dad, but I think that was because he also had fair hair, while my mother was dark. But even when I was very young, I think I still somehow understood that there was no genetic link that tied us together – and that therefore any resemblance people commented on was purely coincidental. It was hard never seeing a trace of myself in another person. I didn't have my dad's nose or my mum's smile or my grandma's hair. It is probably not that surprising that many years later when my own son, Elliott, was born, I just couldn't stop staring at him, trying to find bits of myself in him. I loved it so much when people said we looked alike.

My feelings of being different, of being 'other', were more about my psyche than my physical appearance. I seemed to operate in a completely different way from the rest of my family, and I think that's what always made me question who I was.

I was born on 2 September 1963 at Barnet Hospital in north London, a healthy baby girl delivered to her young – and presumably traumatised – mother, who I later learned was a seventeen-year-old girl named Lesley Sizer Grieve.

It was the early sixties, before things really started swinging, and it was a time of judgement. A time when any single woman – let alone a single teenage girl – was forced to hang her head because of the stigma, of the shame she was bringing on her family by having a baby out of wedlock. Even the most supportive of parents had to be careful who knew about their dark family secret, though Doreen and Ian Grieve were very supportive of their only daughter, Lesley, and did all they could to protect her.

This is where my story starts. I might have been Sue for as long as anyone can remember, but once upon a time, for the briefest period – those ten days I spent at Barnet Hospital – I was Claire Grieve. During those days Lesley fed me, and my great-grandmother knitted for me. At the end of our brief relationship, I was handed to a Mrs Toy, the assigned social worker, along with the knitted shawls from my great-grandma wrapped in brown paper. And after a brief spell in a 'handover' home, a young couple called Freda and John Cleaver, together with their five-year-old son Paul, brought me home. From that day on I was Susan.

I was very lucky to have wonderful adoptive parents, who were kind and loving and always had my best interests at heart. But even so, for me – somehow – there was constantly something missing. That's absolutely not down to anything they did or didn't do, but I think even as a little girl, I understood that my belief system was different. Not that I could have articulated that at the time, but it was, nonetheless, a feeling that I was never able to shake.

My father was a teacher and we moved around a lot, something that I now realise probably contributed to my feelings of insecurity, of not knowing my place or who I was. We lived in Shropshire for a while and then, briefly, in Hemel Hempstead. And then, when I was seven or so, Dad got a job at Gordonstoun School up in the north of Scotland, and so off we went to yet another new life.

My time in Scotland was largely a very happy one. We lived on the school estate, which was huge, over two miles long, and it was wonderful – a real *Swallows and Amazons* childhood. In the holidays my brother Paul and I had the run of the grounds, going off to the woods and building dens. It was our domain and we had a freedom that most children would have envied. At the age of ten I had a moped, as did Paul, and we used to hare off on them for the day, and it would be like, 'Just make sure you're home for five o'clock and don't go near the lake' (though obviously I always did. I regularly came home covered in duckweed. It's remarkable I didn't drown). And that was our life.

In a lot of ways it was an otherworldly existence, and there were even brushes with royalty. We lived at East Lodge, which was by the entrance gate to the school, and the Queen sometimes used to visit unannounced because Prince Andrew was a pupil there at the time. We had an Alsatian called Sam, and I remember one day, my parents were watching the news programme *Nationwide* and I was dressing Sam up in my dad's clothes – his Y-fronts on back to front with his tail through the Y, plus a bonnet and my dad's vest. Suddenly there was a knock at the door and my mum got up to open it. There stood the Queen's chauffeur, his car parked behind him. He said, 'Freda, have you got the key for the gate?' And she said, 'Yes, hang on a minute.' I joined her as she came back and handed the key over to the gloved black hand, which Sam – in his Y-fronts and bonnet – then jumped up and sank his teeth into. The Queen rolled the window down and asked, 'Did he just bite him?' She seemed amused – but I disappeared pretty quickly.

Despite the many good things about life at Gordonstoun, it wasn't all picture perfect, and that feeling of 'otherness' still stopped me from finding security within myself. While the adoption was never hidden from me, my mum had also told me not to let people know about it. This made me feel that it was something to be ashamed of, though that was absolutely not her intention. She understood all too well that people could be cruel, would single you out for being different, and she didn't want that for me. How could she have known that by saying that, it would make me feel like it was a guilty secret, a bad thing to be hidden? Mum is wonderful and has always been incredibly supportive. She did everything for the right reasons, but as we all know, doing things for the right reasons doesn't always mean that they're right. (Ain't hindsight a wonderful thing?) I've discovered that with my own parenting. But I think I've carried a lot of shame throughout my life, much of which probably stems back to the fact I was adopted, that I was trying to fit in, wanting to be part of something and I didn't understand who Susan Cleaver really was.

It didn't help that until I was old enough to join my brother as a pupil at Gordonstoun, I attended the primary school in the local village of Hopeman, and while there were other children there whose parents worked with my father, I was marked out as being different from the beginning. I was very English, I had the 'wrong' accent, and this led to people taking the mickey all the time, calling me '*Sassenach*' (or 'English person'), a derogatory way of reminding me where I came from and that I didn't belong.

In fact, there was one teacher who made it clear they didn't like me simply because I wasn't local, not even Scottish. I was always entered into the verse-speaking competitions, and I often came second or third, or occasionally won one, and each time that teacher would say, 'You have to accept that Nicky Cowham will always get more firsts than you.' So that's what I did. I accepted it. I don't remember ever getting credit for a silver or bronze. I'm sure my parents were proud of me, but I wouldn't have heard their praise anyway; I was too busy believing I wasn't good enough, something that continued long into my teens.

So it would be fair to say I didn't have a brilliant time at primary school, but its location and the freedom it offered kept me going. It was set on a hill, and at playtime we were allowed to go wherever we wanted – except the beach. We ran wild and that was something I loved.

One of the consequences of feeling so insecure was that I hated being alone. Or perhaps it was just too uncomfortable to be on my own, so I needed someone to entertain me in order to avoid feeling the way I did. Either way, I constantly craved company. During our time at Gordonstoun, my mum didn't work. She got involved in the school community, as you might expect: flowers in the church, make-up for school productions (including Prince Andrew in *Simple Spymen*) and various other extracurricular activities – but she was always there when I got home from school or in the holidays. Yet somehow, that still wasn't enough for me.

I didn't always deal with that loneliness very well. I took to wandering around the school buildings, knocking on doors – be they classrooms or offices – and saying hi to teachers or whoever just because I needed that contact with other people. I remember having a friend round to play, and at some point she decided she wanted to go home. I wanted her to stay and planted myself in front of the door to stop her leaving; in the end, my mum had to intervene. It makes me feel so sad to think about that little girl (I'm talking about me, by the way. My friend was released back into society unharmed!).

I wanted to be with my brother Paul constantly – I hero-worshipped him – and whatever he did, I wanted to be there too. I didn't compute it at the time, but because of all of this, I probably drove him mad. I mean, no teenage boy really wants his kid sister following his every move and, understandably, Paul was no exception. God, I probably irritated him to hell, and he was quite rightly thinking, *Stop tagging along all the time*. But I never took the hint. I do remember one holiday at Gordonstoun when he had the job of looking after the creatures in the biology lab. Gerbils, I think. He would regularly go and feed them with my mum and, just as regularly, I would invite myself along. He so clearly didn't want me there and that really pissed me off. Again, I didn't really understand why I felt that way, so I had no idea how to express it. I guess tantrums would have been the obvious outlet, but they were out of the question; our family was quite old-fashioned in that respect, and venting anger or frustration in that way just wasn't the done thing. So, despite being really cross, I kept everything bottled up and decided to go along with them anyway, then made my point by letting out all the locusts. Fair to say that didn't go down so well.

There were a few episodes like that. Nothing too big, no major misdemeanours; I think I was quite repressed, and I was scared of what might happen. So my feelings came out in small acts of rebellion instead.

My childhood was filled with all the 'normal' activities, such as swimming and music lessons, having friends round for tea, but none of those managed to fill the gap within me. I know that if I had said to my mother, 'I'm lonely, I need to be with people all the time,' then she would absolutely have done something about it. But I didn't know what I was feeling, let alone why I was feeling that way, so I had no idea how to explain it to her, or even to myself. And ours wasn't a family where we were into expressing feelings anyway. My parents were loving, absolutely, but the very idea of discussing how we felt… Emotions were a bit of an alien concept. Likewise hugs and other forms of physical affection – though I'd sit on my dad's knee and always have an afternoon snooze with him. In fact, to this day, I find it hilarious to try and hug my mum – it's really not for her and she always resists (hmm, I wonder why I made sure my own child was a hugger from the start…).

One of the best things about my parents being in education was the long summer holidays, when we could all be together as a family, and my happiest memories are of us heading off to the Hebrides, or our favourite, Lyme Regis, in the caravan. It was before the days of seatbelts and I'd stand behind my dad as we sang 'She'll Be Coming Round the Mountain' or 'The Runaway Train' on a loop, only pausing when my mum noticed that I had turned a sickly shade of yellow and then managed to manoeuvre my head out of the window before the inevitable happened. I do recall I was very bad at saying when I felt sick, and on one occasion projectile vomited with *Exorcist* force down the back of my father's neck. But puke aside, those holidays were filled with laughter, with just the four of us, my brother and I running wild, boiled eggs and soldiers for tea and evenings playing board games and cards.

And later, in my tiny bunk bed, I would lie watching my mum hand-sewing some little dresses for my dolls to wear and nod off to the sound of my dad listening to the shipping forecast. To this day the shipping forecast sends me straight to sleep.

My parents were always very frugal. I think back to those holidays in the caravan when on a Sunday night we would always have our boiled eggs and then a Mars bar, just the one between us all. Mum would cut it into eight slices and we'd get two bits each. They would also go through these phases where they might decide to see whether they could survive on £3 for the entire week for everything. I remember my dad once saying to me, 'See my car over there?'

'Yes, Dad.'

'What date is it today?'

'Well, it's Easter, Dad.'

'And do you know when I last filled it up?'

'No, Dad.'

'It was at Christmas. And I've still got three quarters of a tank left.'

They were proper war babies. And because we always grew up with that, I always wanted big shows of affection or big presents. I think as a result of their frugality, Paul and I both became completely the opposite. Not overly materialistic, I don't think, but certainly far less likely to make do and mend. My brother and I have both always had a thing for gadgets, fancy fridges and washing machines – I know, all the glamour. Mind you, until Elliott was a year old, I had a twin tub where I had to hold the drainpipe over the sink.

I think, in her way, Mum knew I didn't like being on my own. She would spend hours with me holding the end of a skipping rope or shell-picking on the beach. My father would concede to be my model when playing hairdressers. I'd wind the wisps of his combover into my mum's curlers and he never protested. He'd be the customer when I played shoe shops with everyone's shoes being brought into the living room and put on display for him to try. And then there was my favourite, the Saturday-afternoon wrestling. We'd watch it and then re-enact it with him as Giant Haystacks, and me as Mick McManus. I loved my parents very much and I know they loved me and my brother equally. There was no way they had an inkling of my inner workings – after all, it wasn't as though I'd worked it all out myself either.

There were things they did get though, my passion for *Jesus Christ Superstar* for starters.

I remember being about eleven and completely obsessed. I had it on my tape recorder and listened to it over and over. My mum would roll up the carpet in our hallway so I could roller-skate up and down, sometimes singing along to 'Crazy Horses' by the Osmonds, but mainly belting out the *Jesus Christ Superstar* soundtrack over and over at the top of my voice. One night, when we were down visiting my grandma, my dad surprised me and took me to London to see the stage show. He said I sat on the edge of the seat singing at the top of my voice to every song while he worried what everyone else was thinking – but he didn't stop me because he could see I was having so much fun.

I guess I liked to perform even then. In those Gordonstoun years I played the violin and at some point thought I fancied giving the piano a go too. I was at that stage where you start to explore all the things you might like to do. I remember when Elliott was a little boy, we bought him a guitar. He decided it wasn't for him. We got him a keyboard. I think he played it once. We tried an art class, all sorts, and kept going, thinking he'd find the right thing eventually. But back then, when I was ten, eleven, twelve, it was a very different time, an era when parents were less indulgent of whims and child-centred everything. When I said I wanted to play the violin because one of my friends did, that was fine. But when I had a fancy for the piano, started it and quickly realised I hated it, I really fucking hated it, I knew that if I said I wanted to give up, my father would just say, 'You've made your bed, now you need to lie in it,' so I was stuck with it. But when it was time to practise, instead of using my fingers on the keyboard, I would use my fingernails to scratch great big marks into the woodwork instead, chip, chipping away. Sometimes I'd get a pencil and poke the tip into the wood to scratch it all the way up, and once I even used my compass to really have a go at it. I made a real mess – yet no one ever said a word to me about it.

Mostly, I think I was looking forward to the day I'd turn thirteen so I could join my brother as a pupil at the school, where there were all number of people and activities to distract me. I was really excited about the fact I'd be with my friends in a place I knew and loved, and there were so many amazing opportunities there. Paul was in the fire service. You could join the mountain rescue. You could sail.

There were drama classes, a whole huge building just for drama. I'd be living in a house with all the other girls. The very idea of it was heaven – although I can see now, of course, that it was a very elitist world which was afforded to us only because our father worked there.

But there was still another year or so to go, so in the meantime it was business as usual: the bad bits, where I kept hacking at the piano, and the good bits, where I had the run of the countryside, although I'm not sure my parents were always overly keen when it came to my pursuits on the nature front. There was a period when I'd take an old trolley and collect rabbits with myxomatosis and bring them home to 'fix' (Freudian, much?). I don't know if you've ever had the 'pleasure' of coming across an afflicted bunny in the flesh, but it's not the prettiest of sights. Oh, and before you search Google Images, let me just say that's an understatement and you're very much better off leaving it in your imagination. Anyway, most of the rabbits were barely alive by the time I 'rescued' them, and I have no idea what my dad actually did with them. I suspect he probably had to put them out of their misery and dispose of them without me knowing.

Nor was that the full extent of my animal hospital. I had pigeons with broken wings in the back of the garage, though they always died. We also had two little chickens which were relatively healthy until a fox got to them. As a result of that, one had a small hole in the back of its neck, and I remember trying to 'cure' it by filling it with papier-mâché. Fair to say I was no Dr Dolittle.

The summer I was twelve, everything changed. My father got a new job at Chetham's School of Music in Manchester, where my mum was to be a housemistress. The plan was for Paul to continue at Gordonstoun, joining us in the holidays, but for me to move south with my parents. And so it was suddenly farewell to the wilds of Scotland, to my dreams, and hello to city-centre living.

Why couldn't I stay put, as planned? Because in their heads I think they believed Chetham's was the perfect fit for us all. A head of boarding role for my dad and an opportunity for his young daughter, whose local music teacher thought she showed some promise. They thought, *She plays the violin, she loves music. This will be marvellous for her.* Meanwhile I've been scratching the fucking piano for fucking months because I hated it so much so, hmmm, maybe not. Again, they were acting with the very best of intentions, as they always did. But instead of this being the great success they had imagined, it became the start of a downward spiral that would see me questioning my place in the world more than ever.

Did I beg to stay in Scotland? I did not. I couldn't. I simply didn't have the voice. I didn't know that you were allowed to question things, and that you could express your likes or dislikes simply never occurred to me. I didn't have any self-awareness at all. That was the problem from the start, that lack of sense of self. And if you have no sense of self, how can you possibly begin to articulate what you need? Truly a lesson for life.

# 2

## I Don't Belong

Many of us find our teenage years tricky. And for a thirteen-year-old who already had issues with attachment and belonging bottled up inside her and kept hidden from everyone else, being in a new home and a new school, mixed in with a hefty dose of hormones, was never going to be easy.

Despite this, I ended up being strangely optimistic about the move at first. I was fairly adaptable, and it felt like a new adventure; I even got quite excited in the end. I figured that I'd make the best of it and all would be well. I was very wrong.

At some point during the first couple of days in my new school, I found myself in a music room with a few other pupils, so I decided I'd play my favourite piece on the piano, 'Für Elise'. It wasn't long before I realised that they were all sniggering and taking the mickey. In Scotland I'd been told I was good at music and that I had talent. But here I was instantly the dunce because all the other kids were prodigies and I was just the girl who'd done quite well in Grade 4 piano and violin, got merits and even distinctions in her exams, but compared to everyone else at the school, was absolutely bottom of the pile. That day is carved into my psyche: the utter humiliation, the shattered innocence of that young girl who had been excited and eager. It broke my soul in two and that's where my vicious, cruel, wicked, demonic inner voice began to grow.

Being average among some of the most talented young musicians in the country was simply something else that made me different. I became consumed with a desire, a need to fit in, but I didn't have a clue how to do it. Desperate to belong, I began to experiment with different personas. I suppose in some ways you could say that was the day the exploration to find myself really started. It's been a fucking long journey.

As women I think we can often find ourselves at different periods in our lives feeling that we don't belong, whether it's at school, whether it's not being in with the in crowd, whether it's starting a new job, or whether it's when hormones kick in, or when middle age changes the way we feel about ourselves. But for me, I think those feelings were always there and exacerbated not only by not really knowing who I was, but also by a dramatic change of environment at a very formative age.

Manchester, where I still live, is a brilliant and vibrant city, but back then, in the mid-seventies, really not so much. In fact, I'd go so far as to say it was pretty grim, with nothing much going on for a twelve-year-old girl. There was concrete everywhere, when I was used to mountains and rolling hills. It was a complete culture shock. I'd lived in a privileged bubble and didn't know this world existed. Despite the fact our parents always tried to keep our feet on the ground, encouraging us to know our place and never to boast, in this new environment I felt like a fish out of water.

My parents didn't want me to be bullied for the fact they taught at the school, and were keen for me to fit in, so they felt that it would be best if I was treated exactly the same as any other pupil. I understand the wisdom in this – those best intentions again – but boarding across the quadrangle from where they lived and having to call them Mr and Mrs Cleaver just like everybody else actually made me feel more different than ever and proved to be disastrous. I was unhappy, I was lonely, and I felt abandoned.

I made friends at Chetham's, but I grew resentful about being there in the first place. Things came to a head when some of the girls in the dorm decided to throw soft toys about in a game of catch. I wasn't there to witness my beloved teddy flying out of the third-floor window and into the River Irwell, but when I found out, I was straight over to my parents in floods of tears. And my dad just said, 'No, no, no, you have to deal with this like anybody else. Off you go.' He was, rightly, trying to make me a bit more resilient, but me being me, I took it as a massive rejection.

Puberty really wasn't the best time to be battling with these feelings either. All the other girls in the dormitory were getting their periods in sync and, as one of the youngest, I hadn't even started mine. I would literally pray, *Please God, let me have my period, let me have my period.* I wanted to be the same as everyone else and being the only one not menstruating just increased that feeling of otherness that continually haunted me.

I didn't know much about body changes because again, this was something we never talked about at home, so my education on that front came from the girls around me. It was pretty basic, though, and I don't think any of us had much idea about mood swings or PMT or anything like that. I didn't even know what hormones were, just that at some point you could stop stuffing cotton wool in your bra because your boobs got big enough. Mind you, I was still in vests at that point, and I remember my breasts starting to grow and my friend saying I needed to tell my mum to get me a bra. I was like, 'I can't do that, we don't talk about those things in our house.' Thank heavens we did have those conversations in the dorm, otherwise when I did eventually get my period, it would have been like that scene from *Carrie*. I was in a gym class, on the horse, clad in the regulation sky-blue towelling onesie shorts (a paedophile's dream), when suddenly someone started hissing, 'Sue, Sue, you've got your period.' I went to the toilet and I was so excited. I was just like the others! At last!

People are so much more open about all this stuff now. Maybe some were then, I don't know, but in our family we really, really weren't. I had no idea where babies came from. I thought they came out of your belly button, which seemed kind of obvious to me – after all, there was a knot there. I think it was my last year of primary school when I finally plucked up the courage to ask. My mother came into my bedroom just as I was going to bed and I just blurted, 'Mum, where do babies come from?' And her response was, 'When you really want to know, ask me properly.' She shut the door and that was that. (And I still haven't worked out how 'properly' was supposed to work.)

In the school holidays we left Chetham's for the house my parents had bought in Poynton, about thirteen miles to the south of the city. I remember that first long summer vividly; I knew no one and was lonelier than ever. Wandering around the woods one day, I came across a stream with a rope swing. There was a group of kids there, so I hung around on the edges of the group, then sidled up to a girl and started talking to her. I was quite good at that sort of thing. I'd had to be, as we'd moved around so much I'd had plenty of practice and a chance to develop the skill. So we got chatting, and after that we would all meet up at the rope swing every day and I was delighted. I thought I'd found my group. This was it. My gang.

At some point in one of many casual conversations, I said, 'Yeah, I'd be better off coming to your school with you guys,' and my new friend seemed very enthusiastic about it. 'Yeah, come to my school. Let's do it. We just need to speak to our parents. You can come and stay at our house.' We must have known each other, what, two weeks? But that didn't stop us forging ahead with our grand plan. Essentially, I told my parents, 'My friend that I've just met says her parents say I can live in their house with them.' I'm sure there had to be more to it than that, but that's my memory of it. So the next minute I'm living with this girl's family – who were effectively strangers – for a term and going to this other school.

Did it work out? Not surprisingly the answer is no. The girl shared a room with her sister, who I'm sure didn't want me in there with the two of them, and that just made things worse. Another place I didn't belong.

Thinking about it now, the whole thing was extraordinary; the fact that my parents and her parents allowed it was astonishing. They were clearly a very decent family and maybe that's what persuaded my parents that it would be okay, but still …

It pretty much went downhill from there. I became even more unhappy, although I didn't really have much of a sense of what that meant. If I look back at my teens now,

I think I was probably depressed, but depression wasn't a word I knew back then, let alone understood. I knew nothing of self-harm or suicidal ideation. I didn't know that people could get to a point where they could decide: *That's it, I want out*. So I just kept on hiding the way I felt, putting on a brave face and finding ways to carry on. I didn't have the vocabulary or awareness to explain any of this, and sometimes it was almost like I was walking round in a trance, trying to ignore whatever I was feeling.

By now Paul had finished at Gordonstoun and was living at home, so it was decided I'd come back and stay there with him and continue studying at the local school. My mum had the day off on a Thursday, so she'd join us at home then, and the rest of the time it was just the two of us. No boundaries. No parents. I was skiving off school regularly and though I couldn't have named the emotions filling my head, I now realise they were mainly hurt and frustration. I remember flying off the handle at my brother one day, screaming at him and smashing a glass door by putting my hand through it. As if that wasn't enough, I threw a pork chop at him across the kitchen and he chased me upstairs and came into my room. I was crying and he gave me a massive hug. But it was clear at that point that something had to change, and in the end my mother had to give up her job because she realised she needed to be there full-time to look after me.

So it was me, Mum and my brother together while my dad was still in Manchester. It meant my parents effectively weren't having a real relationship and my mum had had to leave Chetham's and the job and life she loved; I imagine she was quite pissed off about all of those things. She got an office job instead, nine to five, Monday to Friday, very different from what she was used to. If I put myself in her situation now, I realise it must have been horrible for her, but she never made me feel bad about it. Mind you, in many respects I was a typical teenager, and I was so wrapped up in myself that even if she had, I probably wouldn't have noticed. Her feelings simply never crossed my mind.

There are two sides to every story and mine is no different.

The turmoil, the sadness, the confusion were all part of the hidden workings of my brain. My inner demons, if you will, and which of us can profess not to know how those feel? Outwardly, though, I could not have appeared more different: I was bold. I was brazen. I was empowered. I was never 'broken', but instead I was resilient and strong.

It turns out I was always all right. I just wish I had understood that at the time.

# 3

## The Pursuit of Love

With so many significant changes taking place over just a couple of years, I guess it was inevitable that I found this a very difficult time. The move, hormones, school – they all played their part. I would never want to go back and relive that period; I was very unhappy a lot of the time and my teenage years were very turbulent. It was no one's fault and, as ever, my parents only ever tried to do the best for me, but I was a lost soul.

Had all this happened today, perhaps it would have been different. But this was the seventies, a very different era where no one even had a clue about the concept of mental health. Thinking back, now I feel so sad for my teenage self, for that young girl who always wanted to belong but felt so very lost. As I've got older, I have realised that if you spend your days looking for reasons not to belong, you will always find them; when you decide how different you are from everyone else, you are creating a sense of being separate – but then, as I've said before, hindsight is a wonderful thing (as is therapy, more of which later).

There were boyfriends, one-night stands. I convinced myself that oh, if I do this, they will love me. I was always searching for a way to belong. It was tragic, really, and it breaks my heart to think about it now. There's so much shame wrapped up in my teenage years.

I was very naïve, but my desire to fit in led to a lot of posturing on my part. And that led to me losing my virginity very young. Everyone seemed to be talking about having sex, and I thought if I did it, then I'd be one of them, I'd belong. It was only afterwards that I found out the others were all lying to make themselves look cool.

I was only fourteen when it happened, and it was with a guy who was four or five years older than me. We were at a party, kissing a lot and he kept saying come out to my truck, so I did. What did I know? I thought we were just kissing, with him lying on top of me, but then I felt something and realised. Afterwards I ran back into the house thinking not that I'd effectively had sex without us even having talked about it or there being any form of consent, but, *Oh my God, he gave me attention – it must mean he loves me.*

I saw the guy a couple of times after that, but then he found out how old I was and ran for the hills. A couple of years later we did end up getting together again, though. I guess because he was that bit older, he seemed really sophisticated to me and I was quite into it, but it ended fairly quickly. I didn't really know how to have a relationship, to be fair. I was very volatile, very uncertain of myself. I was just a mess. I guess it was down to that lack of sense of self again, feeling I didn't belong. And how does any sixteen-year-old have a meaningful romantic adult relationship, anyway? I was just searching and searching for someone to make me feel okay, then somebody else, because maybe they would make me feel okay. Because I didn't know how to be okay myself.

So I became really promiscuous and, as if that wasn't enough, I was absolutely shocking at school too. I hated every second of it. I don't remember any teachers that inspired me, and I was never going to learn in an environment where I was determined to kick back against everything. I had so much going on inside my head that I couldn't concentrate on anything else; there was no room left in my brain to absorb facts, so it was easier to switch off. I'd be gazing out of the window, contemplating my navel, sending notes to someone, acting the class clown. I tried to get in with the right people, to speak and behave the way they did so I'd fit in. Not stand out. I did not want to stand out in any way, shape or form. That meant ignoring my natural leanings towards things like drama, which I would really have enjoyed, because it wasn't cool. Not cool at all, so I couldn't be seen dead doing it. I was like a chameleon, adapting to my surroundings for my own protection, and I tried on personalities like coats in a shop.

I made bad choices, dangerous choices. How many of us have found ourselves doing this at a time we feel we are not in control? I'd think nothing of hitchhiking or walking home in the dark, and bear in mind, this was the era of the Yorkshire Ripper. I went to this folk club which operated as a youth club a couple of times a week and we'd be smoking in the toilets. There were drugs there and a few dodgy characters, plus some pretty nasty scraps, with people getting hit. To be fair, that bit did scare me, because it wasn't part of my world and I'd never seen anything like that before. This was all new to me, but I felt I had to fit in to stay safe. My middle-class RP – received pronunciation – accent stuck out like a sore thumb, so I had to very quickly get myself a Manchester accent instead… I guess it stuck.

By this point I was fifteen and I'd been going out with a lad for about a year. He was sixteen and had just finished school and got a job and I thought, *Oh yeah, this is great. This is what you do – have a proper boyfriend.* It was the summer holidays and his older brother came back from the Navy on leave. As my boyfriend was working, his brother and I hung around with each other during the day. I'd come off a horse and broken my wrist, and I remember him coming to the hospital with me to get the plaster on. Anyway, we spent lots of time together and the inevitable happened, so it was possibly not the best time for me to be going away with both brothers and their parents for a week's holiday in Windermere.

So there we were, with me sat in the back of the car in between the brothers and holding one's hand on the left side and the other's hand on the right, feeling, 'This is so exciting. This is amazing. Everybody wants me!'

Cut to the first night in the B&B – quite a novelty for me, as our family holidays were always in a caravan. The boys were sharing a room and I had a tiny one on my own – at least in theory. First the older brother came in and then a bit later my (supposed) boyfriend walked in and found us kissing. And then his parents were at the door telling me I should be ashamed of myself: 'You're shocking, what kind of girl are you?' And me feeling ashamed and just sitting there, not looking at them and not responding. The older brother refused to leave the room, which I was glad about, and then at five o'clock in the morning we packed our clothes, snuck out of the B&B and hitchhiked to the station.

We got the train to Blackpool, where he had an aunt and uncle who let us stay for the night. And they must have lent us some money, because then we found ourselves a B&B on the seafront, where we stayed for the rest of the week. God only knows what my parents thought; the boys' parents had gone round and told them everything. There were certainly words when I got home.

I turned sixteen at the start of September and decided there was no way I was going back to my studies. In those days grades were everything – not that that isn't the case today in some respects, but back then mental wellbeing wasn't something people really thought about– so the decision didn't go down that well, but I had absolutely no desire to conform. So I rebelled, quit school altogether and came out without a clue about what I was going to do and not a single qualification to my name.

That was difficult for my mum and dad, who worked in education, after all, and I felt my father thought I was a waste of space. We didn't always have an easy relationship, though I appreciate now that I didn't make life comfortable for anyone in my teenage years, least of all my parents. Not only did I put myself through hell, I put them through it too, despite the fact that they tried everything they knew to help me. But we'd never heard of terms like 'depression' and 'attachment disorder'. It simply didn't make sense to them that something could be off in a person's thinking.

When I look back now, I feel incredibly proud of my mum and dad, although that's not something I would ever have been able to understand, let alone express at the time. They were truly loyal, decent, honourable people, and if you go on any Facebook page about Chetham's and put in my surname, the stuff that comes up about them both is truly wonderful. Pupils commenting on how my father and mother shaped them. People saying how they were the best house parents you could have wished for, or that my dad was the most influential man in their young lives. They offered stability and safety for many; how painful it must have been for them to see that, for all their efforts, they could not find a way to get me through the tumultuous teenage years smoothly. And to lost, hormonal, rebellious me back then, it just felt like they were so fucking amazing to everyone else's kids and I didn't get a look-in.

So the rebellious streak came to the fore again. I packed my bags and went down to Plymouth to be with the older brother, where we got a bedsit. I mean, what were we thinking? I guess we weren't. It was utterly ridiculous. I was just – just – sixteen, so I couldn't sign on for social security payments. I had no National Insurance number or anything, so I couldn't work either. We lived in a poky room and shared a bathroom and kitchen with loads of other people. He was out all day, and I was lonely and bored. It wasn't the happy life of freedom I had imagined.

Did my parents stage an intervention and come down to Plymouth and refuse to leave without me? No – which I think was actually very wise. They knew me well enough to realise that it would probably only make things worse, and they believed that I would come to my senses eventually. I do remember my mum writing letters and sending the odd cheque, but the whole thing must have been horrible for them. They were right, though – I was home by the end of November. I had loved the idea of the romance: I wanted that happy ever after, at least I thought so at the time – now it seems ludicrous. Oh, and the landlord had also found out my age and thrown us out.

And so it was that my great attempt at a 'love' story came to an end, and I found myself back in Manchester. I was relieved to be out of that situation and back at home – but I was also unhappy, unsettled and trying to work out who I was, where I belonged, once again.

# 4

## From Bad to Worse

I would like to say that after everything that had happened, I had finally learned something from my mistakes. That at last, I had found a sense of purpose and belonging and moved on to a happier, more secure existence. But, sadly, that could not be further from the reality.

Without school to fill my days, I tried various jobs, which I loathed because I couldn't stand authority or hierarchy. I worked in a local supermarket and I hated it. I worked in a fish-and-chip shop and I hated it. I could never stick at anything because I felt, 'No, there has to be more to life than this.'

In my free time, I started hanging out at this wine bar, wanting to be part of another gang. This group of people seemed sophisticated to me, probably because they were all older than I was, and one of them, a 35-year-old man, took advantage of my desperation to belong.

I got pregnant.

I told him.

And he said, 'Don't you even fucking try it. I've got a particular blood type and I will know. And you just need to go away.'

It's not that I wanted to have the child – having kids had never even crossed my mind at that point. But a bit of support for a young, scared girl really wouldn't have gone amiss. Instead he chose to vilify me, cast me out and I was left to deal with it alone.

I knew I wouldn't cope if I had the baby, but then I thought, *Oh God, I'm an evil, awful person for even thinking that*, and my head was all over the place with it all. But I went to the doctor's and arranged a date for a termination without telling anybody, all the same.

I never let my father know about the baby; he had always said that if I ever got pregnant, he would throw me out of the house. Don't come crying to me, that sort of thing, which was very much the stock phrase used by parents of that era. (I know he never would have, really.) So I sorted it all out myself and then went to my mum and said, 'I'm going to tell you something but you have to promise not to tell Dad.' And she was like, 'What this time?' expecting another in the long list of dramas from me. So I said, 'I'm pregnant. This is what I'm doing, this is the date.' And when she didn't shout at me, I said, 'Will you give me a lift? I mean, if you don't want to give me a lift, that's fine, because I've figured out the bus route. I know how to get to the hospital and I'm going in on Tuesday.' But of course she wanted to be there for me. She dropped me off and picked me up and I don't think we ever talked about it again.

Again, this was very much of its time; things were swept under the carpet and people moved on. The idea that you might need to process difficult events, or have time to get over them, wouldn't have occurred to any of us.

Reflecting back now, though, I feel that I was fortunate to have options. I consider how, just seventeen years earlier, at the exact same age, my birth mother found herself in much the same situation but with a very different outcome. Her choices were limited: she could either go through a back-street abortion, with all the risks that would entail, or continue the pregnancy and give up her baby – me – at the end of it. The very idea of being pregnant out of wedlock was shrouded in shame, and while her family supported her throughout, she simply couldn't be seen, and so it meant for months on end, whenever the doorbell rang, she was sent off to hide in her room. When I found myself in a similar position, I had the opportunity to reset and move on. Though it is not lost on me that today – in the twenty-first century – many other women find themselves in the same boat as Lesley over half a century ago. It terrifies me that they are still having to fight for their rights on a daily basis.

I have no doubt that if I had had that child, it would have been a disaster. I could barely deal with myself. I'd never have been able to cope with a baby and it would probably have ended up in care – though, actually, I'm sure my mother would have stepped in to support me, as she always did. But any which way, I never felt the need to mourn it, which, given everything that had happened, was just as well. It was still a massive thing to go through and we dealt with it in a very matter-of-fact way, because that was the way we were. I don't know how it all impacted my mum, because I never asked her. And as before, I didn't have the vocabulary to explain how I was feeling. Now, looking back as I write this, I would say I was in an incredibly low state but then, however bad things were, none of us would have had the first clue what to do about it – and so, once again, it was just a case of: 'This is how things are and now we move on.'

How times have changed – both in general and in my own understanding of myself. Back then the thought of talking to someone – a professional or even just someone who might have been able to help – was something I didn't even know was a possibility. Though even if I had, would I have considered it? Probably not. But I still find it extraordinary now that I simply tried to bury the turmoil. Clichéd though it sounds, it really can be good to talk, even if it's just to get those worries and issues out of your mind and therefore stop them festering and growing inside instead. Maybe saying these things out loud would also have helped to clarify the nub of the problem, or at least give people a clue as to where I was at. Alas, I had no such wisdom back then.

Despite my lack of emotional clarity, I think I had a bit of an epiphany after the termination and realised that I couldn't go on as I had been. It sort of made sense to get away from everything and begin a new chapter far from home. So, six weeks later, still just seventeen, I went to work in Canada as a nanny. I'd just had an abortion, and I found myself looking after other people's kids instead.

I'd been to Canada once before, when I was fourteen. I'd had glandular fever and been quite poorly with it and off school for a while, and my parents had sent me out there for the summer to stay with my godmother, Cousin Margaret, in Ottawa, and convalesce. It was hugely exciting, as I'd never been abroad, and I had a great time. Three years later, when I was lost and looking for options, it seemed like as good a place as any to make a fresh start. And goodness knows, I needed one: I'd had a termination, I'd dropped out of school without a single O level, I had no clue what I wanted from life… I felt like a walking fucking disaster.

It was for all these reasons that I can now see that I should never have become a nanny. I wasn't that good at looking after myself, let alone someone else's children. I didn't know who I was and I had no understanding of anything, really. I just pretended I knew what I was doing; poor kids, I'm sure I was crap. But at least I liked the first family I worked for in Canada, which was something. Ruth was a single mother and had two kids aged five and seven, and we got on pretty well. And in some ways Canada was a good place to be, exciting in that it felt a bit like being in a film. There were drive-throughs where you could get food and you could even watch movies in your car. On Friday nights I used to go to this bar, Jimmy's Bar, at the Holiday Inn. There was a grand piano and twinkly lights and it all felt so glamorous – if a Holiday Inn can ever be called glamorous – and sophisticated. I reckoned this was living!

One day I heard this woman on the radio, a psychic called Geraldine Smith Stringer, and I was fascinated by what she had to say; from nowhere all these questions started popping into my head about being adopted. She was coming to Ottawa and offering readings, and all I could think about was how much I would love that. But it was a lot of money – three weeks' wages. I wanted it so much, but there was just no way – though it didn't stop me wishing I could.

Then one Friday night I was at Jimmy's Bar with my mates, as per. It was really busy and I noticed two women in the corner staring at me. I couldn't work out why. As the evening went on, one of them came over and said, 'I don't normally do this, but I had to tell you that you have this incredible aura all around you. It's like gold emanating from you.' I was a bit nonplussed, to say the least. Then she continued, 'I'm Geraldine Smith Stringer and I want to read for you.' The woman off the radio! I had to tell her I couldn't afford it, but she said she wanted to do it for free. I wasn't going to argue.

So the following weekend I went to the hotel she was at and had a reading, which I recorded on tape. She told me that I didn't realise what I had going for me. I asked her what she meant. She replied, 'Have you ever considered being a dancer?' I had not. She said, 'No, there's definitely dancing somewhere in your background.' Later I found out that my birth grandmother had indeed been a dance teacher,* but with no clue about that at that point, I just said, 'Well, I did go to ballet classes for a bit, but I only had about six lessons because we moved.' I don't think that's quite what she meant. She told me, 'Dancing or acting. It's in you. Have you ever considered it?' Then she said I was adopted but I wouldn't have to search for my birth family, it would just happen. At this point I had no idea what I really wanted and hadn't even considered searching for my birth mother. I also remained pretty sceptical, so I was like, yeah, yeah, okay…

After that, she offered me these classes in reading auras, which again cost far more than I could afford, but she said she wanted me to join as her guest. 'You're very psychic,' she said, to which I replied, 'Am I?' To be honest, I'd decided by now I didn't believe in any of that stuff anyway (although I do love a good ghost story). But I was also curious, so off I trotted to the course nonetheless, and let her teach me how to read auras.

*In fact, both grandparents and my birth mother had been heavily involved in Company of Ten, a well-established amateur theatre company in St Albans, which is still going today. It's where my birth mother met her husband.

You had to get a non-flickering candle in a room – a bathroom with no window was ideal – then look around, but not at the candle. You then had to look in a mirror. You had to do this every day and then you'd start to see the auras. She told me mine was a double blue arc, with gold and green. I can't remember what each colour represented, but it was something like psychic awareness, communication, creativity, stuff like that.

I learned that everyone has different auras around them. Geraldine talked about a man she came across once, the only person she had ever met with a completely white aura. There had been a very famous sinking of a Canadian boat during the war and pretty much everyone on board had drowned or been eaten by sharks. Only two had survived. And when she asked this man with his white aura about himself, it turned out he was one of them. She often worked with families, getting called in to help find missing children and so on, but she was in Ottawa to do radio shows and host a psychic weekend. I was a sceptic, yes, but equally I was fascinated, and that started my interest in finding out more about myself. (Incidentally, I now have a book I bought not long ago, which is written by Geraldine's son – who is a surgeon and a sceptic.)

I came home from Canada for a fortnight in the summer after being away for a year. Mum had gone back to Chetham's at that point, as head of girls' boarding. I told her about my reading and played her the tape and, bless her, she and Dad got out everything related to my adoption and gave it to me. I still have it all. My birth certificate was a short-form one and it was only more recently that I applied for the full one, hoping to see the details of my birth father, but that bit was blank. But there was a letter that said baby Claire's mother had agreed to the adoption and that they could pick her – me – up on the Friday along with their milk tokens.

It felt good to know a little more about my beginnings, but any feelings of positivity about my life vanished as soon as I got back to Ottawa. Ruth no longer needed me, so I started working for a new family with a tiny three-month-old baby who had hydrocephalus and apnoea, which meant she stopped breathing if she cried. She would be like *Waah*, then nothing, and you'd have to rub her belly to get her started again and then she would make alarming gasps. It was hell, stress I probably didn't need right then, and I hated it. I was terrified and really miserable. I found myself alone for long hours at a time with the child, knowing that if I turned my back for a second, it could be disastrous. So much responsibility for a lonely young girl with no sense of self.

I was scared all the time. I was living in the family's basement in a room that only had a tiny window, which I really didn't like. It made me feel like I didn't belong with the rest of the family – yet again I was haunted by a feeling of being 'other', separate from everyone around me, but this time it was mixed with fear. I dreaded every morning, knowing that I would have to go through another day of this. I was scared to put the baby down, even when she was asleep, and I would end up sitting on the sofa with the child on my chest, staring at the TV for hours and hours and hours, because if I put that baby in her chair or in her cot and she stopped breathing and I couldn't get her started again, then it would be my fault. What could I do except watch her every move, feeling alone and frightened? I was desperately unhappy.

I hated every minute, but I was too scared to come home because it would mean I'd failed again. Yet another disappointment from the useless piece of shit that I was. I couldn't fucking do anything right.

I found respite wherever I could. One evening, I went to see a friend in a play that her drama group was doing. On the plus side, it meant that for a few hours I was away from the fear and the responsibility, but it was hard to come up with any more positives than that. The play was atrocious, embarrassingly bad. I was like, seriously? You'd actually let people come and see that? Did you not think of saying sorry, we're not quite ready, let's give it another week? (Stroppy and confused youths tend to make harsh critics!)

But as I sat there watching it, I also found myself thinking, *This is what I should be doing, what* I'm *going to do*. It was my eureka moment. So I wrote to my mum – it was all airmail letters in those days – and said, 'I'm coming home, I'm going to go to drama school and be an actor.' And she replied, 'Don't be ridiculous. You've never shown any interest in acting, never mentioned it at all.'

My poor parents (again). Nowadays, everything is so much more accessible, and being an actor is seen as a more normal job, but back then it really wasn't the sort of thing most people would even think of doing. You didn't just conjure up ideas of what you fancied for an occupation. You went to careers advice at school, and you became a nurse or a secretary. Maybe a teacher if you were academic. But those were the options. Nothing else was offered.

With this in mind, before I went to Canada, my mum sent me on a Youth Training Scheme (YTS) course to learn to type. Off I went to the Sight and Sound college for an intensive three-month course, and it was like torture. You sat there for the first week in a dark room with a screen and a number would come up. There'd be a buzz and you had to press the corresponding number on your typewriter. Buzz, press, buzz, press, and that's how you learned the keyboard. After a week you went into another room where you'd have a set of headphones and hear, 'F. G. D. S...' Boom, boom, boom, letter after letter. And you'd just sit there for eight hours listening to this voice. It was like being brainwashed into learning to type. I mean, it's a very useful skill to have and all that, but because of that experience even now, when I speak, I can often feel my fingers reaching to hit the keys for every word.

But there was no telling me, and once I'd made up my mind to go into acting, that was that – and given my rebellious nature, any attempts to dissuade me simply made me want it all the more. My heart was completely set on it. I couldn't ask my parents to pay the fare, as they'd paid for my flight home only a few months before and I was meant to be there for the whole year, so I borrowed the money and turned up again, thinking how pleased they would be to see me. Instead they were concerned. Here was yet another thing I hadn't stuck at, plus this time I was full of a great plan they really didn't understand. I arrived at the airport expecting this incredible welcome. I was like, 'Hiiiii, I'm home!' waiting for them to say, 'It's been so awful without you and thank goodness you're back.' What they actually said was, 'What are you going to do now? What now, what now?' And I didn't want that. I just wanted them to throw their arms around me and say, 'You're home.'

It turned out – no real shock – that you needed qualifications to get into drama school, so the next step was to enrol in the local further-education college to get that sorted. My mum came with me, and I signed up for a two-year A-level course in theatre studies, to be taken alongside O levels in maths, English language, sociology and art. The maths wasn't a brilliant idea in retrospect, given I was never any good at it. So no great surprise that I didn't last long with that. I also gave up sociology, as I really hated it. But English, well, I don't know who was marking the O level that year, but somehow I ended up with an A. It was a complete and utter fluke and there was no way I deserved it (though I think in those days it also involved coursework and I might have paid someone for a couple of essays). I got a C in art.

I really loved theatre studies, though, and had the most inspiring teacher, Helen Parry, who I'm still in touch with today. I wasn't so keen on the academic side and just about scraped through because of my coursework on Ibsen and Shakespeare. I liked being in their plays, but I really didn't want to talk about them. I didn't want to sit and read; I just wanted to act. But Helen thought I was good and had it in me to become an actress; she gave me the self-belief I needed so badly.

After college came the long-awaited drama school. There was a handful of accredited ones and I applied to them all, including a couple in London, RADA and Mountview, and others closer to home. However, as a mature student it was difficult to get a grant, and it turned out not everywhere was covered. Fortunately, Manchester was, and I happily accepted a place there, ending up in the same year as Steve Coogan. This was my satisfying 'told you so' moment at last!

My mum and dad moved me into a bedsit in Didsbury, a few miles south of the city centre. I had a tiny little room and there was an even smaller bath and shower where every morning the whole wall would be covered in black slugs. It was disgusting and I hated it, and also felt incredibly lonely. After the first term I found a flat, which I was to share with another girl, but she had a breakdown and never actually moved in. It was really expensive for me on my own and although someone else eventually moved in for a bit, I wasn't happy there either. Next I went to live with someone my mum knew from Chetham's, a parent who had students lodging in her big house. There were two other girls who lived upstairs and were doing a teaching course. And while we all got on, no, I wasn't happy there either. I felt like an intruder in someone else's family home. Eventually the three of us moved out and got a flat together.

I went through different phases, that whole 'trying on personalities like coats' thing again, and found myself getting frustrated all too easily; that was always my default, despite the fact that that's not how you achieve anything or get other people on board.

I thought that maybe by being an actress it would be easier to find my voice, but honestly, I'm not sure it was. I was still loud and outspoken; what is it they say about empty vessels making the most noise? Not that I understood that at the time. I had an ever-present need to be validated, to be relevant, to be heard, but I went about trying to achieve these things in entirely the wrong way. Think about it – do you listen, properly listen, to the person who is shouting the loudest? Or to the one who presents their case, argument or whatever, in a calm, rational and considered way? Let's just say that was yet another valuable life lesson that was way in the future for me.

# 5

## It's a Family Affair

Was drama school everything I wanted it to be? I guess the answer is yes and no. It was what I'd desperately wanted and I was over the moon to actually be there at last, but it also made me lose a part of myself, namely the belief that I could act – which wasn't exactly ideal, given the nature of the course. Perhaps this was because those were the days when drama schools used to knock everything out of you, or maybe it was just me, but in my first year I often found myself crippled with self-consciousness. I never talked about it, just kept it tightly bottled up inside, as was my way, but it only compounded the stories I would tell myself about not being good enough and not being able to do it.

But then a director said to me that I'd never stick at it, which maybe did me a favour, as it made me fucking livid and determined to prove him wrong. I was like, 'Just watch me… you'll see.' I mean, there were twenty-two, twenty-three people in a year out of hundreds who auditioned, so I had to have had some potential. And that was always the thing that worked with me. Tell me no and I'll be, 'Yeah, I fucking can.' In some ways that bolshy part of me, which is probably the bit of me that others might find difficult, has been my best friend and kept me going. I won't conform to what anybody else wants me to be. That part of my personality, I now know, has been my saviour.

In my second year at drama school, the casting director from the Royal Exchange, Sophie Marshall, came in to audition a few of the lads for a small walk-on part in their upcoming production of *Oedipus*. I went up to her and said, 'Why are you only seeing the boys? Why aren't you seeing any girls?' She replied, 'Why, do you want to audition?' and I was like, 'Er, yes, absolutely I do.' And so I did, and ended up getting a part, along with Steve Coogan and a couple of the other lads from college.

Little did I know that that tiny role would change my life for ever. For starters, I met my first serious boyfriend through one of the actors and, within a few weeks, moved in with him. He was a lot older than me, and I chose to spend my time hanging out with his crowd, to tie most of my social life in with his, again making myself 'other' by separating myself from my peers, even though I had made friends on the course, some of whom I am still in touch with today. But being part of a new crowd didn't really help. I had this thing that if the people around me were accepting me, there must be something wrong with them (as the quote goes, 'I don't care to belong to any club that would have me as a member'). It was like a weird kind of grandiosity, in a way. I wanted to belong but I would make sure I didn't belong. I'd self-sabotage all the time. Perhaps none of that would have come as any great surprise to anyone who knew me.

But it was another chance meeting that was to rock my world completely.

The cast was a stellar one, including the likes of Eleanor Bron, and on my first day I walked into the green room and there was David Threlfall, who I'd seen in the play *Riddley Walker* some years earlier. I thought he was just incredible, and had even written to him asking whether he could give me any advice. I was a real fan, so it was all a bit embarrassing. He was sat next to Michael N. Harbour, who I recognised from somewhere. Then I remembered he used to present a schools' programme in the early seventies called *Finding Out*. While I was busy putting two and two together, he looked at me and said to the stage manager, 'Oh my God, she's the spitting image of my wife when I met her, when she was about nineteen or twenty.' Although that was something he only told me weeks later.

We became great friends. I was completely obsessed with him and fascinated by his stories about his family, I wasn't sure why. Once the show had opened, someone from the cast had a lunchtime party one Sunday. So we're all there and Michael was sitting next to me, chatting, and he started taking the mickey out of my Northern accent. I said, 'Don't you take the piss out of my accent – I've cultivated this, thank you very much.' And he looked at me and asked, 'Where were you born?' I said, 'I was born in Barnet.' And, unbeknownst to me, his stomach gave a little lurch, and he said, 'What's your date of birth?' 'September the second, 1963,' I said. 'Why?'

He didn't respond, just sat there staring at my hands and going very quiet. I thought it was a bit weird and leaned away to talk to someone else, while – also without me realising – he went off to the nearest phone box, rang his wife Lesley and said, 'I've found her.'

Michael N. Harbour was married to my birth mother.

He and Lesley had two teenage daughters who knew nothing of me, had not the faintest idea that their mum had had another child. She was keen to keep it that way and told Michael not to say anything, not only because the girls didn't know, but also because he had no idea what was going on in my life or whether I'd be able to handle it. Michael, who was always very theatrical and dramatic, apparently told her that he would instead 'leave it in the hands of God'.

So there's me, completely unaware of the momentous shift that was happening a few yards up the road as I sat there eating vol-au-vents, and there's him, rushing back to his car and driving home to Northamptonshire to have a conversation neither of them could have foreseen would come out of a casual lunch party with the rest of the cast. They stayed up all night talking, but Lesley was still adamant that he shouldn't say anything to anyone else about it. She was glad to know I was well and fine, and that was that. She wanted to leave things as they were, as she was worried that I might not be aware that I had been adopted.

Cut to a couple of days later, and my friend and fellow cast member Leonard and I had decided to go for a Chinese after the show. Michael asked what I was up to and I said I was going to get something to eat and why didn't he come too. 'You never come for dinner with us,' I chastised, so he was like, 'Yeah, go on, I'll come,' and off the three of us went to the restaurant. I must have briefly mentioned to Leonard that I was adopted at some point previously, because he decided that this was the perfect opportunity to ask me about it in detail. Out of the blue he said across the table, 'Does it bother you being adopted? Have you ever wanted to trace your mother?' I mean, literally out of nowhere this man started asking all the questions that were in Michael's head, that he desperately wanted to ask but he couldn't. What were the chances? But then my response was, 'Well, I don't know, you hear about people tracing their mothers and finding out they are syphilitic old bags who they wish they'd never met in the end. So maybe it's not a good idea.' And Michael's sitting there thinking, *That's my wife she's talking about.*

I remember he kept trying to pick up this sweet-and-sour pork ball, but it kept falling off his chopsticks and it was really getting on my nerves. I asked, 'Are you all right, Michael?' and he said he was, but needed to go to the toilet. While he was gone, I joked to Leonard, 'Maybe he's my dad,' before adding, 'But seriously, he must have had a child adopted. When he comes back, go to the loo and I'll try and find out what's going on.' So when Michael returned, I kicked Leonard under the table and off he went, and I said, 'Is everything all right, Michael?' And he went, 'I need to talk to you, but not here.' The dinner ended soon after. Leonard went home and I got into Michael's BMW, and he drove me back to my place. We sat in the car outside the flat and he just turned to me and said, 'If I told you I knew who your mother was, but you could never tell anyone, what would you say?' And I said, 'If you've got something to tell me, then get in my flat and do it properly.' (Bolshy as ever!)

What happened next is a bit of a blur, but Michael always told me he remembered that when we got in, he went and sat in the lounge by the bay window. I went into my little galley kitchen and got a stool, and I put my stool right near the door to the lounge but also near the front door, basically as far away as I could get. I guess I was terrified about what he was going to say. So I said, 'Okay, what?' and he answered, 'You are my wife's daughter.' Ever the sceptic, I said, 'Really? Well, let me tell you something, I know what my name was and my mother had an unusual middle name. So come on, then.' And he went, 'Your name is Claire Grieve. Your mother is Lesley Sizer Grieve.'

I've got no idea what happened after that, how the conversation ended or what was said when he left. But the next day he reminded me that we had to keep this to ourselves, and so we carried on for a few days with this secret. People at the Royal Exchange started to talk because they thought we were having an affair or something. I was twenty-three and he was forty-something and it all got really awkward. So even though it wasn't what Lesley wanted at that point – she was still trying to process it herself – it was clear that something was going on, so when Michael went home that weekend, they sat their two daughters, Kate and Emma, down and then told them all about me.

When he told me that was what he'd done, I thought, *Well, that's not fair, if you can do it then I can too, so now I'm going to tell my family*. I called my brother Paul and told him everything. He drove to meet me after the show that night so we could go back to my parents' house in Poynton to tell them, even though it would be pretty late by the time we got there. I waited for him at the theatre but he didn't come in, so after a while I went outside to look for him. He was there at the bottom of the steps and I said to him, 'Why are you down here?' He said, 'Well, I didn't want to come in. I didn't want to make things awkward for you.' Even now that breaks my heart. I was just like, 'Oh my God, you're my brother. You're my big brother. You're more important to me than any of these people.' And it just really got to me, though I didn't voice anything like that.

We didn't communicate like that in our family. But to this day, I still hate that he felt that. Hate it.

So we go to my mum and dad's and I tell them. My mum goes, 'Oh my God, that's amazing. I cannot tell you the number of times that I've thought about that woman. When it's your birthday I've wondered how it is for her, is she okay. I hope we've done right by you.' She demonstrated true generosity of spirit and was really interested. My father said, 'It's half past eleven. Couldn't it have waited until tomorrow morning?' Typical Dad: he could always be relied upon to react in his usual down-to-earth manner. But he wasn't an unemotional man, in fact, quite the opposite – he couldn't get through certain films or pieces of music without tears in his eyes.

A few days later this amazing letter arrived from Mum. It said, 'It's such exciting news to hear about your friends…' *Your friends* – she didn't know what to call them. '…and I've enclosed some photographs of you as a baby. I've taken them out of the albums, so I would like them back if possible, but please show them to her.' And she'd written things on the back of each picture, with dates and this is Sue at such and such an age or in such and such a place. It was so, so generous of her. The letter ended, 'Please tell your friends that they are welcome any time to visit us.'

In the meantime, Michael arranged for me to meet Lesley. It was at this hotel in Northenden, a disgusting, rotten, horrible place by the flyover and I thought, *Well, this isn't very glamorous*. It was after the show; I'd asked her not to come to that because I didn't want to look around the theatre and see her. I thought, *I just can't do that*.

Michael and I got in the lift and went up to the ninth or tenth floor and as we got out, he said, 'You're on your own now.' I was reluctant to meet her without him, but he insisted. And it was like that scene in *Poltergeist*, where the child is trapped with the devil in a bedroom and as the mother runs towards the door, the corridor gets longer and longer and longer. It felt as though I'd never get to the end of it, and half of me just wanted to run away, while the other half was glad that this moment had finally arrived. Eventually I knocked on the door and she opened it. And we hugged and then we talked, though again, the memories beyond that are a total blur. It's only through Lesley's diaries that I can recall anything about the rest of that evening. How we talked and ate and drank and laughed until dawn, when she realised I was exhausted and needed to sleep. She said she couldn't stop staring at me – though forced herself not to do it, as she didn't want me to think she was loopy.

I arranged for us all to go to my parents' house, and my mum, bless her, had laid out a lovely spread and my dad had got the projection screen up and all the family slides from my childhood. They talked through the slides: this is when we went here and this is when she did this. She used to love doing this, that and the other. It was like they were trying to fill Lesley in on the last twenty-three years or so, which was such a generous thing to do. I'll never forget how kind they were. But I think it was pretty overwhelming for Lesley, all a bit much. As she wrote in her diary, it was the first time in twenty-three years that she had been able to talk to me in the knowledge that I could hear her, I could respond, and at times it felt like she was dreaming. She described how she wanted to express her love for me but was afraid the intensity would frighten me off. It was all very full-on for both of us.

At that point, we decided that we were going to tell the cast because there was still all this whispering going on. Lesley came to the show and at the end Michael ordered some champagne and after the show that evening made an announcement that everyone should go to the green room. He was very theatrical, as I've said, so he made this big speech about here we bring together mother and daughter, and I remember thinking, *Oh, fuck, you know, this is embarrassing*. Everyone was completely stunned, like their mouths just hit the floor. No one could believe it. I just remember them all sort of coming forward and then giving me and Lesley a hug and like, what the actual fuck is this? What have we just witnessed? And from then on I became known as the Royal Exchange Theatre baby.

Funnily enough, the way we met turned out not to be the only coincidence in our story. One of the first people I was introduced to after Lesley and I came into each other's lives was Helen Worth, who plays Gail in *Coronation Street*. She and Lesley had lived together when they were younger, and she was one of the only people who knew about me from the start. She's godmother to one of my half-sisters. What were the chances of the two of us ending up working together for almost a quarter of a century? I loved that when I did become a colleague on the cobbles, she would drop things into conversation such as, 'You were so like Lesley in that last scene,' or, 'Goodness, you do have your grandmother's decolletage.' You couldn't make it up.

Then there's my two half-sisters, Emma and Kate, who've both been in the business too. Kate is a voice actress who played Wendy in the children's show *Bob the Builder*, and so when Elliott was small, she was in my living room all the time. The relationship still catches me out even after all these years. We went on a cruise recently and shared a cabin for ten nights. We'd never been in close proximity for that long before, and I found myself recognising things in me that she did. We liked the same things. We'd order the same food. We'd approach things in the same way. That familiarity was a novelty to me, and it fascinated me because for so many years of my life I didn't look like anyone, behave like anyone, see any similarities.

Emma was incredibly generous when I tried to find out more about my birth father. I had my DNA done and put it into one of those websites to try and find any connection, and she added hers too so that any links on our mother's side wouldn't confuse things. (I still haven't got anywhere with that search, but maybe one day…)

The whole thing has been a great experience for me and answered a lot of questions. I also feel very fortunate because they welcomed me with open arms, whereas a lot of people who trace their birth families can be disappointed or greeted with more rejection. I think that's why I probably would never have gone looking myself. In some ways, Lesley, who died at the start of the pandemic, felt more like an extended relative, a cousin, than anything else (and my mum will always be my mum), but I'm so very grateful that we found one another – and that she and my mum became friends, visited, went to stay with one another too. She meant a great deal to me.

Of course it was all pretty strange and confusing at the time, but it did make me think back to my stay in Canada several years before and I realised that Geraldine Smith Stringer had been completely right. I never did have to go searching for my birth family, because the universe just dropped them in my lap, in the most unexpected and unlikely of ways.

# 6

## Moving Forward

In some ways, meeting Lesley completed a piece of the puzzle of who I was, but in others this new relationship continued to unsettle me. By the time *Oedipus* finished, my head was pretty messed up and I couldn't really cope with college for the rest of that term. Yet again my mind was filled with a whirl of conflicting emotions, and yet again it meant that there was so much going on in my inner world, so much I was trying to figure out, that there was no capacity left for learning, which was exactly what had happened when I was at school. So the summer term of that second year was pretty much a write-off.

In the holidays, Michael and Lesley invited me to stay with them in Cornwall. They would go there every summer for a big family get-together in this stunning manor-type house belonging to a relative. It was a village called Trebetherick, where the poet John Betjeman had lived and David and Samantha Cameron had a place at one point – in fact, all the relatives' kids had been pallbearers at Betjeman's funeral, and the relative was now busy putting together a collection of his artefacts to exhibit.

The gathering was large, and I found it the most awkward thing ever. With the bedrooms full of an assortment of relations who were part of this yearly tradition, I ended up sleeping in what seemed to be a library. Propped next to my head was the large wooden cross that had marked Betjeman's grave until the tombstone was erected, so that wasn't creepy at all. I just didn't feel comfortable. I didn't belong. I was so out of place, a cuckoo in the nest.

Weirdly enough, years earlier Michael had been in a BBC series called *The Cuckoo Sister*. It was about a family with two daughters and then another child who had been brought up in London and so had the wrong accent and just didn't fit in. She was the cuckoo sister who infiltrated the family – and I suddenly realised that that was me. It was like we were living the whole thing out for real, although obviously in this case it was my cultivated Northern accent that stood out from everyone else. Any which way, I was different. And the otherness, again, was enormous.

I was supposed to stay with them for a fortnight, but after just three or four days, I just couldn't hack it any more. I rang my mum and said, 'It's not working, I need to come home,' and she was great. She said, 'Right. Well, you don't have to explain yourself to anybody, and if you want to come home, you come home.' And because there weren't any trains at the right time, she paid for me to get a flight from Newquay instead. I wanted to go straight away, and Mum knew I'd be too embarrassed to say this, so I think she must have spoken to Michael and said, 'Oh, Sue needs to get home for something. Could you please drop her at Newquay? And could you make it this afternoon, as something has come up and she needs to be back today?'

And so I left and after that I didn't see any of them for quite a while. It had all happened so fast and so unexpectedly, and we needed some space.

It had been all too easy to get completely swept up in the story of my birth at the beginning. It was such a huge thing, and I became the talk of the town. Everyone's reaction was to celebrate this extraordinary event. It was a miracle! Not to mention the fact that it all came about when we were working on *Oedipus,* which, let's face it, was the perfect backdrop to this very theatrical story. It seemed uncanny that there we were in a play that seemed to reflect so many of the themes that were then being played out in real life.

- Fate and free will: was this discovery ordained by God?
- Emotional guilt and shame for having done something terrible. Some might say that could apply to Lesley (not that I ever saw it that way myself, I should add).
- Sight and blindness. Had we been blind to the truth about our own lives?
- In the play, finding out the truth was Oedipus' undoing – could this potentially be the undoing of me and/or Lesley?

So many similarities! There was also the question of whether ignorance is bliss, and whether the past is best left alone. This felt hugely relevant to where we were. As did action versus reflection, and the fact that when Oedipus saves his people from the plague, he becomes his own judge and punisher.

It all felt too much for me and for Lesley, even though for Michael it was a dream, and he loved to regale people with the story of how it all came about and how amazing it was… 'And then this happened. And then this was marvellous.

And it was all ordained by God.' It was a great dinner-party speech, to be fair (though to him it was far more than that, and before he died he said that bringing us all together was one of the best things he had ever done). But other people seemed to forget that there were two human beings in the centre of it all. There was me. And there was my birth mother, who until I appeared had been seen by everyone as a paragon of virtue, whiter than white and who had now been forced to admit to not being that at all. She was 'damaged goods' and there was a lot of shame around that, and I felt the shame of her shame. I think, in a way, we fed off each other. Behind the headline of the miracle story, real people bore their scars. Shame, denial, secrets – they all impacted on us both deeply and that in turn had an impact on those around us. Not that I noticed it so much in my own family, though I was extremely sensitive when I don't think I needed to be. Friends said to me. 'Be careful, this will be incredibly difficult for your mum and dad.' But when I did enquire, they responded with huge munificence. They were happy for me and pleased that all the questions I had could now be answered.

When my mum told me that there wasn't a day they didn't think about my birth mother, about how she was and whether they had done right by me, it was extraordinary. It made me realise too late that my parents' love, although not expressed by grand gestures and bold statements, was a quiet, steady and generous love. There was never a need from them to be the best, the most loved. When people are not treated as possessions, you do not take ownership of another person's heart, and me exploring a relationship with Lesley was never a threat to them. I understood then that they had always been the constant in my life, a solid, safe haven, and my love for them and my brother – as well as, later, my son – is one example of pure, unconditional love.

My third year at drama school was more straightforward, and on the whole I enjoyed it. We did some nice plays and I knew for sure that this was the world I wanted to be a part of. Others might have judged my eureka moment in Canada as yet another of my whims, but for once I'd got it right, and this really was the place for me. Despite my lack of self-confidence during my studies – and I was now in a place where I doubted myself even more – I always managed to find some fun, and there were some happy times during those years. Whether I was playing the rebel, or partying, or having other adventures, I'd get out there and find joy and fun in all sorts of places. I went backpacking, hitchhiked to Paris, did all the things young people were meant to do.

There was also my new relationship, which was very different from any I had had in the past. Yes, there was a big age gap, but he was settled, sorted and, somewhere deep in my subconscious, I think I believed that being with him would take me away from the really intense situation with Lesley.

However, things weren't straightforward with him. We were at very different life stages. He was a really lovely guy, but he was a grown-up, and although I was twenty-three, emotionally I was still a kid. Not only that, I was a skint student, and he ran a successful recording studio. There were a lot of problems in our relationship and I think that most of them stemmed from the fact that he was established, with a career and a business, and what did I bring to the table financially? Absolutely jack shit. That was an issue for him. I ended up being extremely, extremely overdrawn, not in the regular overdrawn student kind of way but because I felt I had to keep up. He was like, well, you're not providing as much as I am. And yes, I was aware of that, but how the hell could I be expected to? You know, it was his house. It was his property. Everything was his. And I didn't like that, so I would make sure that I bought food and did whatever I could. As a Christmas or birthday present from my family, I'd ask for money that I could then use as a contribution towards the carpet or something else he had bought for the house because I just so wanted to make sure that I was doing my bit. The thought of being with somebody and not providing… I hated that feeling. But I really couldn't keep up. I wasn't ready for that sort of life at all, but I wanted to belong, so I put my face on and just got on with it.

Don't get me wrong, there was some good in the relationship too, but it was hugely imbalanced and it made me vow, even at that young age, that I would never, ever, ever allow myself not to earn my own money. I never wanted to be in that position again where I was beholden to anyone, let alone a man. Even before I finished drama school, I'd take holiday jobs to make sure that I had my own cash coming in.

Many of us will remember that first serious boyfriend. When we became so wrapped up in the feeling of 'us' that the strong bonds of friendship we'd made before were instantly disregarded or pushed to the side. This is what happens when we lose ourselves in relationships. In that heady, and I stress hormonal, falling-in-love stage, you connect so strongly that there is a danger that their world becomes yours. But when this happens, you unconsciously start leaving the other people in your life behind. You put your partner's wants and desires first. The dynamic of being with somebody considerably older, as I was, means that you start to defer to them, as they have more life experience and you trust that they must know better than you. You adopt their belief systems, their politics, their practices without figuring out who you are and what you believe. We want to be loved and accepted, but sometimes that need becomes so strong that we do ourselves the greatest disservice: we lose sight of the dreams we have for ourselves. The longer you spend with that person when you haven't got a strong picture of who you are, the bigger the temptation is to become who you think they want you to be.

If this is your situation, it's important to remember that strong relationships should be built on mutual respect and support for each other's individual growth. I learned that it's very important to set boundaries, to hang out with my friends, to love who I am and figure out what I believe in. We do not have to earn love. If you find yourself in a position where you do, consider it the biggest early-warning system that you're ever going to get, and you'd be wise to listen to it.

If you'd asked anybody what I was like at that time, they'd probably have described me as the life and soul. But on the inside, it was a very different story. Even though I had found my calling, had a huge piece of the puzzle of my life explained, and was in a steady relationship, things were complicated. The inner workings, as ever kept hidden from everyone else, kept filling my head with negative thoughts, and the cruel, wicked demon, the one that insisted I had no talent, that told me I wasn't good enough, was still sitting firmly on my shoulder.

# 7

## Role-Playing

Searching for approval from others or people-pleasing can start very early, as I found out to my cost – not that I was aware of what I was doing or why I was doing it at the time. As children, we seek approval from our parents, teachers, authority figures, friends. Later we look for validation from partners, lovers or colleagues. But before any of this, what we really need to do is seek approval from within ourselves. I had no idea that that was the case. After all, it wasn't something anyone had ever talked about and nor was it something that we learned how to do at school. It took me well into my forties to understand how important this is and that we all need to be taught to connect within ourselves and become our own champions.

Seeking validation outside of ourselves is exhausting and often fruitless. Other people have their own agendas, and half the time they themselves are searching for life's answers too. Certainly, my efforts did me no favours, yet I still firmly believed that I needed validation from everyone around me and didn't understand that constantly searching for approval and inclusion from the outside is a never-ending journey, and that way madness lies. I had no clue that I had been looking in the wrong places and that to find our own approval we need awareness and non-judgement to open the door so we can notice our patterns and change the roles we've handed to ourselves. And as it took me a very long time to learn any of this, as a result I look back at so many events from my younger years and see how differently I might have done things – or at least stopped beating myself up when things didn't pan out as I wanted them to.

We all play many roles in our lives, often unconsciously, believing this is how we should behave as women, as daughters, mothers, sisters, wives and more. By my early twenties I was not only a daughter, a sister, a student, a friend, but also a girlfriend and a recently discovered birth daughter, and I'm not sure how well I knew how to be any of those things, especially the latter. In fact, I didn't get the sense that I was playing the role of daughter for Lesley at all. I felt that we were just getting to know each other, and we were both fumbling around in the dark and not quite knowing how we were supposed to be with each other. What did other people expect of us? Were we upsetting anybody? Were we doing or saying anything that my newfound half siblings might find uncomfortable or wouldn't like? And then there was Michael – we had been very close before all this came out, but he was her husband, so where did this leave our friendship? I felt my allegiances moving all over the place and tried to be hypervigilant in order to ensure I was what I was supposed to be to everyone else.

Inevitably that ended up extending into my relationships with my parents and my brother too. I went into protection mode, where all I could think about was whether I was doing right by them. I don't think for a moment that any of them were aware of this – in fact, Paul was living away by then – but inside my head was that voice saying, 'Here you are at the heart of yet another drama. That's always been your role, hasn't it? Sue is always at the heart of the drama.' And so my focus was all about how I could make up for that.

There is often a lot of expectation about how we should stay in our lanes and not rock the boat, which was not something I had been overly successful with in the past. But then the paths put before me when I was younger – by school, by society, even by my family – were not ones that appealed in the slightest. Breaking away from expectation to forge our own paths can be a hugely positive thing, but there is also a danger that it can leave us adrift – especially if you are someone who has never quite managed to rid yourself of those constant feelings of self-doubt and not belonging. But was that going to stop me? You guessed it.

Through my boyfriend, his friends – his best mate was a floor manager at Granada Television (GTV) – and the people I met at college, I found myself living on the periphery of a new and exciting world that I very much liked the look of. My first introduction to working in TV was as a part-time typist one summer holiday when I was a student, not in itself remotely exciting, I admit, but the environment completely fascinated me and it was a way to find a foothold. I started in the typing pool at Granada and went on to do several little stints as a production secretary, though goodness knows how, as I was absolutely appalling. In hindsight, I think a lot of this was that I couldn't stand being around an industry doing something other than what I wanted to do, i.e. act, but secretarial services were never meant to be my forte and God help any man who said, 'Put the kettle on, love.' I'd simmer with rage before responding, 'Fuck off. I'm not your love. Get your own fucking tea.'

I could not stand being told what to do. My problem with authority again? Very possibly. But even through the darkest days of my angst and issues over the years, I had never, never seen myself as a victim. I was upfront. I was bolshy. I would stand my ground. And I wasn't going to be walked on by anyone. That included the arsehole men – and it was always men – who I met in my Kelly Girl temp agency days, when I'd be sent to accountants' or architects' offices and the like. I fucking hated it. Every job I got seemed to be full of really sexist men, and I wasn't having it. I had to do loads of filing and used to take my revenge by making sure I stuck everything in the wrong place where they'd never find it.

I felt much more comfortable in the broadcast world, though I do remember wasting time – apologies, GTV – wandering the building trying to stave off the boredom. Often I'd walk past make-up rooms and dressing rooms, and on occasion I'd bump into the likes of Bob Monkhouse, who had a penchant for walking around in nothing but a smart robe and socks with garters. He was charming, but that certainly wasn't the case with everyone, and I was told never go into the dressing rooms with x, y or z. Everywhere you'd go, talk was rife and people knew the wrong 'uns. But there was no chance of me doing that. I already knew that I wanted that dressing room to be mine and had no interest in anything else.

I progressed to doing a stint as a petty-cash buyer on the sci-fi sitcom *Red Dwarf* for the BBC. Again, this proved to be disastrous, not least because I can't add up. In my very short tenure there I managed to spill a two-litre tin of gloss paint in the passenger side of the BBC company car. (I immediately drove to my parents, who spent a good two hours helping to mop up and disguise the damage.) The calculations of my spending were wrong on a daily basis, not least because I frequently lost my receipts. As you can imagine, they loved me.

I then moved on to a production company as a secretary. Halcyon Productions was based at Liverpool's Albert Dock, next door to the *This Morning* studios. Marian Nelson and Rob Rohrer were two very respected producers from Granada Television, and they were both very tolerant of me and my uselessness as a PA, a PA who so obviously had her heart set on being an actor. They would hold casting sessions for their various productions and I would be silently screaming, 'For God's sake! Hello, cast me! You'll get a lot more for your money than having me as an incompetent PA.' (Years later, Rob directed a few episodes of *Corrie* and said that they had followed my career with interest. It was lovely to finally be directed by my former boss.)

Given the proximity of our offices, we also pitched ideas for *This Morning*, and a very young, inexperienced 25-year-old me had an interview with the creator and then editor, Dianne Nelmes. I hadn't a clue how to pitch and didn't even really know what it meant. I just came up with an idea to make over other people's gardens, as I hadn't seen anything like that being done before. It was the 1980s, but while I now like to think that I was ahead of the times, the closest I ever got to *This Morning* in the end was dropping off some flowers at Judy Finnigan and Richard Madeley's house, as they lived not far from me. I was furious that neither were in when I knocked on their door, as I'd thought that maybe they would discover me.

(In another weird twist of fate, it turns out that Richard and Judy bought their Cornwall house off my sister – and that she became godmother to their children, but this all happened years down the line.)

Still a penniless actor who needed a regular wage, I started a job at Action Time, producer Stephen Leahy's iconic game-show company. I worked as a researcher, trawling around the country interviewing potential contestants for *Wheel of Fortune* and *Win, Lose or Draw*, to name but two. I did enjoy my time there and I loved it when Steve came up with a new idea and we'd all gather in his office and try it out on a Monday morning. But deep down I was still restless, still waiting for my big chance, and everything else was a matter of filling in time, distracting myself until that moment would finally arrive. (At this point I should probably thank Steve Leahy for turning a blind eye whenever I photocopied my face and other parts of my anatomy on the photocopier.) Caroline Aherne was also working there as a secretary, and we would often talk about our futures and about the fact that neither of us ever had any plans of staying behind a desk. We left around the same time. It had been very much a means to an end for us both. She was already performing on the Manchester comedy circuit as Mitzi Goldberg and then Sister Mary Immaculate, and I secured my Equity card – at last – from the Octagon Theatre, Bolton.

This was huge for me, as back then Equity was a closed shop – you needed to have an Equity card to perform professionally – and it was incredibly difficult to break into. I tried to get gigs all over, working men's clubs and all of that sort of malarkey, but those cards were like gold dust and getting one was the biggest hurdle to face for anyone coming out of drama school. Repertory theatres like the

Octagon got two cards a year to give out, so my chance of a role in a music-hall-style Christmas show was about far, far more than just appearing in the production itself. It was the key to unlocking my future as an actress, a future I had dreamed of and one that I hoped would be the answer to all my prayers.

# 8

## Settling Down

Once I had my Equity card, the world was my oyster – or at least that's how it felt – and I was free to take on whatever came my way. I was offered the role of Sharon, the nanny in Alan Ayckbourn's *Man of the Moment*, produced by the Library Theatre Company, and I jumped at it. James Quinn was in it and I'd heard a lot about him. He was a great actor, but I knew he didn't suffer fools gladly, so while I was excited, I was also a bit nervous and thinking, *Oh gosh, I hope he's all right.*

It was a great production and they even built a proper swimming pool on set for the bit where the nanny drowns the father, i.e. James, because he's horrible to her. Which was interesting, because James couldn't swim and I had to hold him down under the water. In fact, there was a classic line I always remember where Sandra Maitland, who played the wife, calls out, 'Sharon, Sharon, where is Mr Parks?' And I had to say, 'I'm standing on him, Mrs Parks.'

And that is how I met my husband, James Quinn.

I was twenty-six, twenty-seven at that point, and he was four years older, so much more my own age than some of my previous boyfriends, and he was the best thing that could have happened to me at that time because he saw that I could act. In fact, he was my biggest champion right from the start. He'd say, 'You're bloody good. You just don't realise that you're good. You've got to believe in yourself.' And, of course, I didn't believe in myself: I didn't believe I had anything to offer, so this was exactly the encouragement that I needed. More than that, it showed me that the relationship I'd been in for the last four years wasn't giving me any of those things, which is why I got together with James.

For a long time, the two of us were incredibly good for each other. We really helped each other and were each other's biggest champions. And I admired him so much as an actor. I still do. In some ways we were quite different; while I had spent my life craving company, James was very insular and really loved spending time on his own. We were both very creative and so we did lots of creative things together. Along with a couple of others, we wrote a show called *Miner Damage*, which we played at the Labour Party Conference during the miners' strike. We were in a comedy impro group called Comedy Express. They were heady days. That's not to say that there wasn't the odd blip, but we weathered those, and then we got married and it was great.

I'd never really wanted children, but when I turned thirty it was like a switch had been flicked and all I could think about was how much I wanted a baby. I really, really wanted to be a mum and so we had Elliott and he's the best thing that has ever happened to me, ever. But I found the love I felt for him absolutely terrifying; it was paralysing to suddenly have this person completely reliant on me and I thought, *I'm a fuck-up, I don't know who I am, I'm going to fuck him up*. And these thoughts filled my head day in, day out, leaving no room for anything else and I completely lost my creativity, although it's only now that I can see that that's what happened, that the fear took over my inspiration and my imagination.

I remember saying after I had Elliott that no one tells you when you have a child that you lose your innocence. I felt so overwhelmed by this little bundle, so worried that I wouldn't be able to protect him from the world. For a period I couldn't even watch the news as everything became so hugely personal.

I was scared that he would feel like I had felt as a child. Scared that I would screw him up. Scared that something would happen to him. I worried about the fact that James and I were both actors and how were we going to make it work and how could I handle my career and bring Elliott up the way I wanted to. As a result of this, my worries took centre stage and my trust in myself diminished further. I felt like I was floundering while James was clearly still growing; he became more focused than ever. He did a master's in poetry, joined poetry groups, wrote poetry, and performed poetry. His creative side was thriving and mine seemed to be dormant and we were on different paths. He was very good at being on his own, but I really wasn't and I found being alone with a small child really hard.

I was haunted by the idea that I wasn't getting it right, petrified of something going wrong. I was anxious all the time. I know now that many women feel the same way – in fact, friends have since told me it was exactly the same for them. But I didn't realise that then, and it can be quite a lonely place thinking that you are the only one in this position.

I remember when Elliott was very little, just a few weeks old, and the health visitor came round for one of her checks. There was me expressing various anxieties about a million different things, and she was like, 'Well, that's the problem with you geriatric mothers. You don't just get on with it. You think too much.' I mean, 'geriatric mother' – what the actual? I was thirty-two! I wanted to slap her – though obviously I didn't. But to give her her due, there was probably an element of truth about the rest of it. Maybe we get older and wiser and see the realities that lie ahead. Maybe a younger woman doesn't question everything so much. But then that had been my problem my entire life. I overthought everything. And did her comment stop me doing it? Not a chance.

There were times when I was even scared of my beloved son. Really scared of him, thinking, *Oh my God, what if I can't settle him? Then what? Why is he crying so hard? What if he stops breathing like the baby in Canada?* I was hostage to my thoughts and that made it very difficult to step away from them into the here and now, to enjoy new motherhood and go with the flow.

Things got a bit less fraught as he got a little older, but I was always anxious and never felt that I was enough for him. It might have been easier if I had shared my worries and talked to James about them, but I didn't. I couldn't. I just didn't know how, so yet again I kept those feelings firmly hidden inside me.

We both adored Elliott and were really close to him. He was the apple of our eyes. But all the while my anxiety festered, unbeknownst to anyone around me. Because this was the thing: I was known for being loud and outspoken. If I wasn't happy with something, I'd shout it from the rooftops. But what no one realised was that if it had anything to do with my own frailty, I would never say a word. I'd just keep on keeping on, being Elliot's mum, being James's wife and fitting work around life at home.

I was lucky that my career was going well and that James was – and still is – hugely supportive. (It brings me immense joy and pride that while we are no longer together, we are still the best of friends and will always have each other's backs.) I leaned on him in those moments when I needed somebody behind me. But I think what always saved me and what drove me forward professionally was partly the rebel in me and also the fact that the alternative was too unbearable. Working in a shop or going into an office just didn't feel like an option for me back then. Not because there is anything wrong with doing either of those things at all, but because they were places I didn't want to be, and so I got bored… and that, in turn, left too much space in my brain for overthinking and overanalysing. I needed to keep busy, to have fun. I had to be stimulated, be creative. I did try to put my typing skills to use again and found it unbearable, though probably not as unbearable as my employers found me – and to be fair, it wasn't where my talents lay. I'm very different now; I can find enjoyment and happiness in anything and can absolutely see the benefits of a job where you can switch off. But back then? Oh my God, the terror, the thoughts of how unfulfilled I would be – though in reality, it was all about doing something to shut those voices in my head up, about not being able to sit comfortably with myself.

I was working on a Harry Enfield comedy series when I got the call for *Coronation Street*. I'd been doing *Dinnerladies*, the Victoria Wood canteen comedy in which

I played Glenda, as well as various other jobs, and I was down in London a lot. I wanted to be home more and hated leaving Elliott all the time, so the very idea of a great role that was filmed close to home was like a dream come true. I went off for the interview at Granada and there were quite a lot of people going up for the same part, including several I knew. I walked in and had the meeting and afterwards rang my agent and said, 'I've got that.' I mean, cocky cow or what? Then an hour later, they called me and it turned out I had.

I felt like I'd hit the jackpot. It was a fantastic role, and so brilliant from a practical perspective too: it meant I could be there for Elliott in the evenings to give him a bath and read him a story. No more crazy late nights or constantly having to be away from home. This was almost unheard of in our business, and such a privilege. It offered the security of a regular wage too, so it was a no-brainer in that respect. I had found it really hard to cope with the insecurity of having a child while not knowing where the next pay packet would come from.

But alongside this professional stability came uncertainty on the home front. There were already cracks in my marriage. James was still very much into his poetry, and writing and exploring all these things. I was working full time and being Mum when I got home, and the old feelings had begun to creep back; I felt increasingly empty for all the same reasons I always had throughout my life. I realised that even within a relationship you can feel very lost and lonely. That's when I started having an affair with Brian.

Brian was a BBC lighting technician who'd come over to ITV to work on *Coronation Street*. We got together. And it was every bit as messy as you might imagine.

# 9

## Life on *The Street*

I feel very lucky to do what I do. I've always worked to live and have never been hugely ambitious for the sake of ambition, although I knew I wanted to make a living out of doing something I loved, and I feel very fortunate to have been able to do that for so many years. Looking back, I do find it interesting that such an insecure teen would choose a life as an actor, which is so often insecure in itself and where there's no certainty. A job like the one I have is a rarity and I'm immensely grateful that despite the many performances I have given on stage and screen over the last four decades, the professional role that has defined my life for quarter of a century – which makes me feel incredibly blessed but also incredibly old – is that of Eileen Grimshaw.

*Coronation Street* has been a constant in my life for so long that it feels slightly off to admit that I was never a fan growing up. Not because I didn't like the show, but because I didn't really know it existed until quite late on. My father was a real we-only-watch-BBC person. We never watched ITV. He didn't even like me watching a cartoon, and I used to have to fight to watch *Scooby-Doo*. I think my nana used to watch *Corrie*, but we never did. I knew some of the characters by osmosis – Bet Lynch, Hilda Ogden, Ena

Sharples, people like that – but that was it. I think my father really wanted me to be on *Last of the Summer Wine* because it was one of his all-time favourites.

I didn't have any idea that it would be a long-term thing when I took on the role. I don't think any actor goes into anything thinking, *This is a job for life*, even if there is potential to become a long-standing character. It's out of your hands. But here I am, over two decades down the line, still in Weatherfield and still very much a Grimshaw.

Eileen and I are very different in many ways, although equally there are elements in her that I recognise in myself. But then, Eileen is every woman. Everybody knows an Eileen or thinks they know an Eileen. You only get what she wants you to see, but that's the case with so many of us too: we have our public personas and the rest we hide. It's the nature of who we are.

Eileen is confident. She's dependable. She's fearless. She doesn't take any prisoners. I realise now that she is everything that I actually wasn't, but that I pretended to be. In fact, I think people would have been shocked at how different we really were in that respect, but then they had never seen the inner workings of my brain, only the mask I wore to hide them. I never allowed anyone, even the people closest to me, to see the truth.

Eileen is a fighter. She's a single mum who's had to fight for her kids. She goes through all the same battles that so many other women have had to go through and it's this that makes her hugely recognisable. As I've played the role through my midlife years, it's been interesting to see Eileen change and me with her – in a good way, I think. Eileen has helped me to understand that our problems are universal, no matter what background you're from, because, ultimately, they all come down to the same things: relationships, family, money, health. All universal. We are all the same. Though in real life we do have to find ways to deal with our problems that might be different from the way they are dealt with in a soap. Less hair-pulling and brawling in the street, for starters.

I look at Eileen and think, *There's a woman who has not put boundaries in place*. She's filled her house with waifs and strays; she never says no. She puts everyone before herself and forgives appalling behaviours in others. It's given me perspective on my own life and made me realise I have far more boundaries than she does.

Or do I?

In truth, I've always been a huge rescuer – just like her – and it's only now that I'm recognising that that's not necessarily a good thing for the person I'm rescuing or for myself. Some people have called me impulsive over the years, but I've put a lot of stock in my intuition and that has served me quite well. However, boundaries are an area I've had problems with, so perhaps I'm more like Eileen than I've given myself credit for. When I see someone else who is in trouble, it's often been the case that I feel the pain *with* them as opposed to feeling *for* them, and this has led me into rescue mode. I feel their pain and I want to support them because I know that I needed help years ago, and subconsciously I guess I'm trying to fix that. But in doing so, in rescuing other people, I have found myself overwhelmed and burned out, which is nobody's fault but my own. I've put so much into looking after other people that it has stopped me from looking after myself. Learning to put boundaries in place is a work very much in progress for me, but at least I now understand that supporting from the sidelines can be far more healthy than being in the game. But I have rescued so many people over the years. I've even had people living in my house because they've split up with their partners. So there's a prime example of why one shouldn't get wrapped up in other people's problems which, now I think about it, does sound exactly like a *Coronation Street* storyline to boot.

Over the years, the cast of *Corrie* has become my other family. And like all families, there can be some personalities you find more difficult than others. But at the end of the day, there's an almost unbreakable bond. You've got everybody's back. You would defend everybody to the hilt. The fact that it is very much a family relationship is one of the reasons I've stayed so long – because it has helped to fulfil that whole sense of belonging that I so often struggled to find.

While I have the greatest of fondness for Eileen, I've also done what I can to keep her life separate from my own. As far as I'm concerned, she is my job, and before I come home, I metaphorically stick her in the prop cupboard and leave her at the office. But obviously it's not always that simple, and often I find that when people look at me, they are only ever able to see her. I get it. She is a familiar face who showed up in their living rooms and how would they even have an inkling as to who Sue Cleaver is? A well-known film actress once said to me, 'The thing is, Sue, that I'm only in something every couple of years, so when people see me walking down the street they might say, "Oh God, there's so and so," but that's it. But you are in their houses three times a week, so it almost becomes a personal relationship and people do think they know you.' And they do. They say, 'You must come round to ours. You'd fit in really well – you're just like one of us.' I just thank my lucky stars that Eileen is one of the good guys and I don't play a baddie; Simon Gregson (aka Steve McDonald) found people would come up to him and try and beat him up.

I suppose a positive of all this is that in some ways I have been able to hide behind the character, which has meant it's been easy for the real me to stay firmly under the radar and hidden in plain sight. But right from the start I found the whole fame thing excruciating, absolutely and utterly excruciating. Fame, to me, is a by-product of being an actor and it is not something I ever wanted or courted deliberately. These days there are so many reality shows, and through them reality stars whose entire aim is to be famous, but certainly when I started out in the business it was never something you searched for. For quite a few years if somebody came up to me in the street or wherever, the inside of my stomach muscles would all tense up and I'd be thinking, *Oh God, don't come over. Don't come over. Don't come over*. It absolutely terrified me when people did. I'd be thinking, *I've got nothing to offer you. I don't know what to say. I don't know what to do*. And it probably came across that I was a bit brusque, but it honestly wasn't me trying to be difficult. It was fear, pure and simple. Scratch the surface and you'd find my confident exterior was paper-thin.

I think there was only once that it really did make me smile. I'm an ambassador for the children's charity When You Wish Upon a Star, and every year we take a bunch of kids to Lapland. I love doing it, and spending time with the children is always entertaining and a lot of fun. A few years back, there was one little girl whose mouth dropped open when she saw me; she was clearly trying to compute how I could be standing there in front of her. I went over to say hi, and she asked, 'How did you get out of the television?' I said, 'Don't tell anyone but there are some little steps so I can slip out down the back. But that's our secret.'

The rest of the time, deep down, I was really shy and completely embarrassed. And I just couldn't imagine why anyone would want to come over to meet me. I didn't like being recognised at all and I really wished that when I first went into *Corrie* I'd done what Julie Hesmondhalgh (who played Hayley Cropper) did. She had a wig, and so nobody knew who she was until she opened her mouth. I asked myself a million times, why didn't I do that? Why didn't I have a wig? Why? I wanted Sue's life to remain Sue's life. I was shocking. I didn't handle it well at all.

I'm sure that a part of this was also due to the fact that when my son was younger I wanted my main focus to be on being his mum and not doing anything that might make life harder for him. He never watched *Coronation Street* because that was when *The Simpsons* was on, but he did really hate it if people came up to me when we were out. ('But you're *my* mummy.') When he hit his teens, he literally begged me not to come to parents' evening because he didn't want people to see me. His hormones were all over the place and the last thing he needed was his mother sticking out like a sore thumb. I got it, and I knew I had to go with it, even if it did sometimes hurt my feelings.

It can be difficult enough being the child of a celebrity without tell-all headlines or salacious gossip all over the tabloids, so it was something I wanted to stay well clear of. Bear in mind that this was also the period when phone-hacking was rife, so everyone was constantly on tenterhooks, but the thought of him reading '*Coronation Street* star caught peeing on the hard shoulder of the M6' or whatever was, well, you can imagine.

The whole press intrusion thing at that time was terrifying. I saw what it did to people and witnessed the horrific things that some friends went through. They'd get a phone call on a Saturday morning saying, 'Just a heads-up that on Sunday they're going to be running this,' and they were powerless to stop their private lives being splashed across the tabloid front pages. I saw people's relationships implode and I was petrified by it. So when some nice member of the public came up and said, 'Hi, I love your character,' I found it quite threatening. I was like, *Oh my God, what are they going to do, what do they want of me?* I was completely paranoid – we all were – and I just didn't know what to do.

All the same, there were definitely times when the edges of life on screen and off screen became slightly blurred and there was the odd occasion (only the very odd one, mind) when the Corner Shop on set would be the place to stop by if we'd been filming late and I knew there was nothing at home for dinner. Checking the date on a jar of Bolognese sauce and deciding that as it was only a month out of date, it was worth the risk. To be fair, it never killed me. Nor did the fact that back in the day we all used to smoke in the Rovers. Forget health and safety – I guess the haze of cigarette smoke only added to the ambiance of a real boozer. We had Bass shandy on tap, though I think at one point in the past it had been actual beer, which was probably stopped for obvious reasons. Often during the summer we will encounter a swarm of fruit flies that have been attracted by the sweetness of the shandy and it's not uncommon to see the bar staff swiping a tea towel with gusto around the pumps.

*Coronation Street* brought a real turning point in my life, not only in the way that it offered consistency and security, but in the fun it brought too. It allowed me to build brilliant working relationships which have lasted for decades, and being able to have a laugh during a long day at work has proved to be an absolute tonic.

Simon Gregson and I had a secret book on the set of Street Cars, a big A4 lined thing that was supposed to be part of the set dressing. For years we would write shocking notes in it to one another, to be discovered by chance while filming a scene. I would often come across a ridiculous picture of myself 'by Simon aged 7' while I was mid-sentence during a take and inevitably end up corpsing and having to do a retake.

There was great excitement all round when Robert Vaughn came to join the show for a spell in 2012, though unfortunately I had never seen *The Man From U.N.C.L.E.* I do, however, remember seeing a man wearing green overalls outside near the studio garden and casually went over to enquire when the best time was to dead-head a hydrangea. How was I to know he wasn't the gardener? Luckily he was extremely kind in his response and not remotely offended.

Then there was the big storyline of the relationship between Eileen and Paul, played by Tony Hirst. Paul's wife Lesley had Alzheimer's and we explored all the ramifications that entailed. There was a scene where I was trying to placate her and she hit me. We had a stunt advisor and had spent some time practising our manoeuvres, but unfortunately during a take, Judy Holt, who played

Lesley, got a bit carried away and an upward punch made contact with my face. I don't remember anything else but apparently I dropped like a stone, out cold. There was a deathly silence and I came round to the sound of Tony laughing like a drain and Judy beside herself because of what had happened. I was promptly carted off for a scan, but my pain was not in vain, as the take got used and the accompanying sound was indeed me being knocked out. Okay, maybe that bit wasn't such a laugh for me at the time, but at least I can see the funny side now.

There are definitely times when it feels quite surreal to do what I do, and never more so than the time we filmed the iconic fight between Eileen and Gail Platt. It took several hours, and it was a very damp and drizzly day (I know – rain in Manchester. Shocker). After ripping several handfuls of hair out of the back of Eileen's head, Gail ended up straddling her in the middle of the cobbles, and after what felt like an eternity of lying on the cold, wet stones with someone sitting on top of me, all I could say was, 'What a fucking stupid way to pay the mortgage.' (I also recognised the irony of us doing this, given our shared history.) To this day it is not lost on me that I actually make a living by choosing something from the dressing-up box, putting on some make-up and playing with my friends.

I find it extraordinary the weight *Corrie* carries worldwide, the currency the show has in places you would never expect. I've done personal appearances in Canada with Tony Hirst and in one place sold more tickets than Bob Geldof had the night before. Also, while in Canada, I got into a helicopter for a sightseeing tour and the pilot decided to hover and tilt so he could get the ground staff to take the perfect shot of him and me for his wife, who was a fan. I have even stood in the Sweihan Desert in the United Arab Emirates and had an extremely handsome Arabian man, resplendent in dishdash and Louboutin sneakers, approach to have a picture with me. I have been in the Okavango Delta in Botswana walking with elephants and had a ranger approach to say, 'Hello, Eileen.' Sometimes, it appears, reality is very much stranger than fiction.

# 10

## Mother Love

During those early days on *Corrie*, things were going well on the work front and I had the stability I had always craved. But away from the cobbles I had a broken marriage and a new relationship, with all the turmoil around those that you would expect, and there was so much going on in my head that at times it was hard to know whether I was coming or going. Sometimes the noise was deafening, but even then, through it all, I was still able to identify an almost primal urge to make life as good as it possibly could be for my beloved child.

Yet the worry and anxiety were as strong as they ever had been. I loved Elliott more than anything on this Earth, but that only increased the pressure of 'needing' to get it right and doing everything I could to stop him ever feeling the way that I had as a child. Rationally, of course, I now understand that sometimes these things happen despite what a parent does or doesn't do. But back then my monster continued to whisper – shout – in my ear that I wasn't good enough and that he deserved more.

Motherhood was and still is the greatest achievement of my life but it's only with hindsight that I realise that it also changed me into someone I didn't really recognise, and I was oblivious to the fact that I was losing the essence of myself. I'm sure that this is something that many other women will identify with, likewise the self-imposed guilt that ends up being a staple in our lives. We worry whether we are relying on the childminder too much. That we aren't prioritising the right things. I would end up feeling bad because I was looking at my watch, thinking, *How much longer do I have to play this ridiculous game that he wanted to play?* Because I had only managed to push Thomas the Tank Engine round the track twelve and a half times before my attention drifted. Because I got irritated when he was irritated. Because I felt guilty at getting angry when he was having a fit because I hadn't given Elmo, his googly-eyed monster toy from *Sesame Street*, a spoonful of yogurt. Because I hadn't satisfactorily smashed the two trains coming in opposite directions on the track and said, 'Oh, choo-choo gone,' and spoiled the game. Because I prayed that his eyes would close and he would go to sleep and I would not have to read *We're Going on a Bear Hunt* for the fifth fucking time in a row. I wasn't going round it or over it or under it – I was going through it. I felt guilty for not being like the mum in the TV adverts, for not being enough, for not being perfect, for being a crap mother. Sound familiar?

There were things that I was good at, though. Every day I held my child close. I looked him in the eyes and told him I loved him, that he was my special boy. I created adventures for him, made more and more complicated cakes for his birthday at his request, not least the challenging dinosaur swamp cake. I queued for hours to make sure he got the Tracy Island playset he wanted so much. I sat up until 4 a.m. on Christmas Day placing hundreds of stickers on the Micro Machines toy that Santa was bringing. I made omelette sandwiches on demand, day or night – he still talks about that. And I loved him in a loud, big, emotional voice.

My approach to motherhood was almost as a managerial role. I thought I was listening to my son, but in fact I was listening with hyper-alertness to the possible things that could harm him so that I could problem-solve them before they even happened. I was looking into the future rather than living in the present. I don't think I lived the right way at all at the time; it was fear-based parenting and I wish I'd known then that there were simple things I could easily have done to change this.

It probably didn't help that around this time I also found myself navigating an unexpected event which threatened to engulf me with a profound and lasting grief. It was December 2001 and my dad was due to have a triple heart bypass, not something any of us were unduly worried about until he left me a phone message saying, 'Hi Sue, just to let you know that I've been fast-tracked in for the operation. Isn't that wonderful news? We're heading in this morning, so I guess I'll speak to you after I've had it done.' The minute I heard this I tried to call him back because I wanted to say, 'Don't get fast-tracked in – prepare yourself and prepare your body properly.' But by then it was too late and the operation was already underway. I went down to see him in Birmingham and everything seemed to be good. He'd made a load of friends on the ward and was chatting away, introducing me to everyone.

A few days later he was home, and we were all relieved and delighted that he was feeling so well. But only days after that my mum rang to say things were not good and an ambulance was on its way. The next thing he was in intensive care, and they told us he had VRE, a superbug, and they decided that they needed to take out the staples from the operation because of the infection – which would mean putting him into an induced coma for twelve days. I spoke to him on the phone, and he said, 'Night-night – I'm going to have a nice sleep and I'll see you soon.' But when it came to the twelfth day, they couldn't bring him round. It was my first ever Christmas Day with Brian. Elliott was with James and it was just the two of us. The turkey was in and we were watching *It's a Wonderful Life* when the phone rang. I always know when something bad has happened with my mum because she puts on this very, very high and proper voice, which almost makes it sound like what she has to say is happy news; it's her default. The news was very bad.

She told me that he had an internal bleed in his stomach, but they didn't think he was well enough to withstand being taken to theatre. So then they decided to do the procedure in the intensive care unit – were we happy with that? We said, 'Go for it,' which then became our family motto: just go for it. So they did and he came through it. But on the Boxing Day, my brother rang and said, 'Dad's not well,' and so I was straight back to the hospital before returning to Manchester to host a party I had no appetite for but which my mum and Paul refused to let me call off. 'Dad would be furious if he knew you'd cancelled the party because of him and let everybody down. We're here and everything will be all right.'

On the morning of 29 December I got a phone call from Paul to tell me that things weren't great but I shouldn't come down because it was a long way to go and he'd keep me posted. But I felt separate from everybody, both mentally and physically, and couldn't bear the feeling of otherness creeping in, so I told Brian I couldn't wait to hear what was going on and I needed to go there and then. We got in the car early that morning and went back to the hospital – and I'm so glad we did.

The doctor came over to explain that Dad was on dialysis and it wasn't working. I remember Paul saying, 'Well, can you not bring in another dialysis machine to use instead?' But they said, no, that machine was working perfectly. It just wasn't working for him. Poor Dad was riddled with infection, and they gently told us that they thought it was time to turn off the machines that were keeping him going. There was this awful, awful pause where we all just looked at each other. It seemed to go on for ever until the doctor took that away from us when he said, 'I'm going to make the decision to turn these machines off. And you can, of course, disagree with me.' But we didn't. I will be forever grateful for that simple act of kindness, that sensitivity which meant we didn't have to say those words ourselves.

It was still devastating, of course. At one point I went outside for some air. I was crying and although I was clearly very upset, a woman asked me for a photo – which for obvious reasons I declined. She called me a bitch! The downside of fame hitting even at my lowest ebb.

Later we sat with my mum and my brother on one side of the bed, me and Brian on the other, Mum and I holding hands as we waited for Dad to stop breathing. And my mum started talking. She said, 'I'll never forget the day that we brought you home. We picked you up from the foster family, who were such a lovely family. He was a musician in one of the big London orchestras, I think, and they had a daughter who was about fourteen or fifteen. We knocked on the door and this girl was there holding you. And we walked in and your dad just instantly took you from her arms. He just scooped you up and he took you off and had a little chat with you in the garden.' And as she was telling that story about me, the nurse put her head around the corner and said he was gone. That conversation brought everything full circle and truly gave me a sense of belonging.

I loved watching my dad with Elliott when he was very tiny, having one of his little chats. It meant so much and I felt immense sadness that those days were now over for good. But I did start to find that motherhood got a bit easier when those baby and toddler days had passed. The primary-school years are the easy part, really, when you are the centre of their world and you have some control, you can protect them – and being able to protect them is the greatest thing. But the transition to senior school is a different thing altogether. You're no longer there all the time and that's really not great for an anxious mum like me.

Education was not a priority for me in my teens; I was always far too consumed with trying to find peace in myself, searching through others and always finding myself lacking. And as a parent, I never wanted my child to experience that. You take all the good things you remember as a child, and to that end I was determined that my son would be told a hundred times a day how much I loved him. That he felt special. But I also vowed that I would make sure he wasn't moved around from school to school, that he would know where he belonged, that he would never have to search for his place in the world. When I reflect back, I am sure that the constant moving around over my formative years contributed to my lack of self, that it led to those feelings of insecurity and low self-esteem. It impacts a developing child's sense of who they are, as they are never able to fully integrate into the pack and, as a consequence, spend so much time feeling 'other'.

I wanted more than anything for my son to be part of a community. I knew that school could be traumatic, and I aspired to do everything in my power to protect him from that. I remember very quickly selling a house I loved and moving half a mile down the road to ensure he got into the school where his friends were – not necessarily the best school, as I recall (in fact they had just gone into special measures), but it was about having his people around him. That mattered to me so much. It makes me incredibly happy that he and his best friends, Andrew and Dylan, who I like to think of as my other kids, celebrate the fact that they are still as close aged twenty-eight as they were when they were two.

My priority has always been my son's mental journey, placing emphasis on the things I wanted to fix from my past. Did I get it right? Of course not. He wasn't me. His life experience was different from mine. He needed attention in different areas. But I strongly believe that the majority of parents do have the best of intentions and that we do the best we can with what we have at any given time. We can only do what we know, though, and the bits we got wrong we need to learn to leave in the past. It's so important to forgive ourselves for the times we have found ourselves lacking, to celebrate the things we've got right, and to realise that every single one of us is fallible. This is the very essence of being human.

I wasn't a mum who spent hours over homework or worried about grades; I was more anxious that he felt secure and safe. I also knew that learning resilience and being able to engage with anyone without prejudice was more important than getting a B in maths. He didn't enjoy senior school and scraped his way through his GCSEs, but I knew he was smart and intelligent and that when he was ready, he'd find his way, just like I did. And he did it in spades with an honours degree and, more importantly to me, with integrity, spirit and a wicked sense of humour.

The toughest part of parenting was like everything else for me – overthinking. I worried constantly about whether he felt loved, whether he was happy, and these feelings only intensified with time; no one tells you how this all gets harder the older they get. You can keep them safe until the time you can't. When they reach an age that reminds you of all the things you did wrong at that point, you worry about their judgement. Will they make better decisions than you did? When are they old enough and wise enough to make the right choices? But there is only so much you can do to point them in the right direction, and that feeling of impotence tortured me at times.

It's not surprising that I made some really unhelpful, impulsive decisions in my own teens. I spent a lot of time carrying bad feelings about those times, but now I choose to put them behind me. It helps to know that good people can still make bad decisions, especially teenagers. Teenagers' brains are mostly at fault. The amygdala, the area of the brain that is responsible for immediate reactions and responses, is much more developed than the frontal cortex, which controls reasoning and helps us think before acting – and which develops much later. So adolescents' brains effectively work differently from adults'. As I am sure many of you have done, I tried to keep this awareness in mind when being a parent myself. Though – and I am sure you will be familiar with this too – good intentions have a tendency to make themselves scarce at trying times.

And then your kids are suddenly grown up. I found this stage so difficult, and it was hard for me to see my son for what he was: a smart, emotionally intelligent, capable young man (if you're reading this, Elliot, and I'm making you sound more perfect than you actually are, never forget, as your mother, I know where your dead are buried).

Letting go is really not easy. You work hard to give your kids roots and wings, but when they actually fly the nest… It took me ages before I felt comfortable enough to put my phone on silent during the night, just in case he needed me. I still find it hard, but he is twenty-eight now. The truth is no one gives you a manual on how to navigate this transition smoothly. You know it's time to let them go, but we have been programmed to protect them. And then overnight we're expected just to release them. I couldn't find a happy balance to do that.

Luckily we have found our way through that period now. We have very similar personalities and have weathered our storms, but we thrive, with love and humour the cornerstones of our family. We are lucky that we've always talked, and this has helped me realise that I am no longer in the management role. I'm now in a consultancy role – and only if he requests it.

For many of us, this stage of life, of letting go, coincides with menopause (or perimenopause), a time when we suddenly seem to be viewed differently by society as a demographic. Dismissed, diminished – it's almost as though we are being told that our contribution to the world is over. Add this to the feelings of no longer being needed as a parent – or being edged out at work, or facing one of the other (many) challenges that are thrown at middle-aged women – and it can make it a really, really tough period to navigate.

For me all of this added up to a perfect storm, a cumulation of all the things in my life that had contributed to my feelings of insecurity, of vulnerability, of being lost. I found myself in a sink or swim situation. Did I accept that this was how life had to be and continue a downward trajectory? Or did I take steps to make things better, to move forward to a brighter new future?

I'm pleased to say that I chose the latter, and while I'm very much still on the journey, at last things are good. I no longer feel lost but have found a confidence in who I am. And at sixty, I'd say that's pretty good.

# Part Two

# THE MATURE SISTERHOOD

# 11

## Changing My Mind

All the things I have revealed about my life I have done because I think it's important to explain where I was in my head when I reached middle age, and why things needed to change. Now I would like to do more of a deep dive into the work I have done and the journey I've been on to reach a better place, to become the happiest I've been in my life to date. I appreciate, of course, that we are all different and that the advice and experiences I will share here are by no means one size fits all. But I hope that they will resonate, and will at least provide jumping-off points to find what works for you.

This part of the book is about self-knowledge, which I think you can only really gain through life experience. This (at last!) is a definite advantage of being middle-aged. We have been there, done that, bought the T-shirt and learned a whole lot in the process. And it is through this knowledge we can bring about positive change.

For me, the root of so many things I needed to work on came down to chronic overthinking, which, as I have already mentioned, had been a major issue in my life since childhood. It took me many (many) years to realise this, despite the fact that it has ruled my life and I have no doubt that the addictive tendencies which I struggled against for a long, long time stem from this overthinking. I would overeat not because I was hungry but because I wanted to – needed to – shut out the noise in my head. I'm sure many of you will relate. I would also drink wine to quieten my thoughts. I'd engage in risky (for me) behaviour to distract myself. Overthinking made me believe that I was lacking, and my energies were taken up with searching outside of myself, as that's where I thought happiness lay.

The noise in my head that just would not shut up and go away has meant decades of trying to find diversions – even as an adult – be it seeking out company to avoid being alone, obsessively planning stuff for the weekend, organising an event, having a party, planning a holiday. To be at peace I had to constantly be distracted, to always have something to look forward to. By Thursday I'd be panicking about not having any plans at the weekend, something that would take up my thoughts. In the days before shops were open, I hated Sundays with a passion. Everything and everybody was having a day of rest, which was absolute torture for me, as it meant I faced hours and hours of being alone with my thoughts. I would try to come up with anything to stop that critical voice having the space to shout so loudly that it often felt as though I had this sort of 'thought tornado' that just took over everything. It wasted so much time and energy.

There have been so many times when I have found myself completely wrapped up in this way. When I've been thinking, thinking, thinking. When I've been trapped by those thoughts – and, more to the point, I've truly, truly believed them. I have hung on to those beliefs for dear life, even though they were not serving me well.

There's a brilliant analogy by Aaron Turner, a practitioner of the Three Principles (more on this later), which says listening to your thoughts when in a low state of mind is like listening to recommendations from your financial advisor when he's drunk. Would you trust his advice?

Of course not.

I have IBS – irritable bowel syndrome. I wake up and I have a pain on the upper-right-hand side of my abdomen, which is not unusual. I notice it. I think, that's okay, it's in the present. But instead of sticking with that, I then start to project into the future. Oh God, what if it's not actually my IBS? Maybe I should google it. Pain in the upper-right quadrant: gallstones... pancreatitis... Oh God, what if it's none of those and it's actually liver cancer? As soon as I allow that thought storm to take over and jump into the future, I've set myself up for a really nasty experience for absolutely no reason other than the fact my IBS is playing up today. Thoughts will always come and go, but we can choose whether we pay attention to them or not.

I should add that it goes without saying that I don't want to downplay IBS in any way. It's a condition that can make life really tough for many people. But I know that I can make my own symptoms worse at times by stressing about them, to the point I can't think about anything else, and this has been a hugely valuable insight for me. When it's bad, it's bad, but I really don't need to make the good days bad as well. You can apply this to all sorts of other situations too.

We don't often say, 'Oh God, I feel amazing today.' But how often do we say, 'I feel awful (or rubbish or fed-up)'? The difference is that if we feel happy we just feel happy. If we feel sad, we start to think about how we feel, we start overthinking. We get wrapped up in our thoughts and the content of our thoughts, and then we start to believe them. Of course we all have times when we feel sad or angry or find ourselves in a low mood. But these are most likely the times that our thoughts become destructive, unproductive or unreliable – essentially, we kick ourselves when we're down. We focus on the content of the thought. We obsess. (By the way, when you're reading this chapter, you must not think about lemons.) We start to hang on to our thoughts. We start to believe what they are telling us. I have days where I've felt overwhelmed: when writing this book, filming *Corrie* and preparing for a National Theatre tour, for example. When this happens, my thoughts naturally lead me to search for affirmations that today is a crappy one. I'll look for confirmations that I'm inadequate; I'll make comparisons with others and find myself lacking. I will clutch on to these feelings for dear life.

So how do we get rid of those nagging, unpleasant thoughts? (Remember, don't think of lemons.) We will always have thoughts popping into our heads, but those thoughts are neutral until we give them life and value. So it really is what we do with them that matters. For example, I recently went back into doing theatre after twenty-five years away. This was daunting enough in itself, even before I started to consider that I was only going to have five days' rehearsal before I opened in the show. And then:

Thought pops up... *I have five days to rehearse and learn this musical.* I then start layering that thought with: *I can't do it. What if I forget my lines on stage? What if the audience notice? What if they have to stop the show? What if it happens when the producer is in – I will never work again. What if, what if, what if...?*

You can see clearly what is happening here. I've got to a point where I am experiencing all the unpleasant feelings of anxiety and stress from one single thought that I have layered with imaginary threats. Instead of just observing that initial thought, letting it go and watching it melt away so I could get on with my day, I have taken a seat on an emotional rollercoaster and as a consequence I'm now getting everything that a rollercoaster has to offer: lurching stomach, dizziness, fear. We are the creators of our lived experience.

My dear friend Sarie came up with this very helpful analogy. You are in a meeting when the fire alarm goes off, and in the moment it startles you, until someone tells you it is just a test alarm. You are relieved and carry on with your meeting. The alarm doesn't seem as loud and you can even carry on with your conversation while it's still ringing. It doesn't seem as loud because you're not focusing on it, you're not questioning what it means. It might still be loud but it is no longer significant, and the noise will lessen until it miraculously disappears. And it's the same with thoughts when you give them your attention and try to analyse them rather than simply noticing them and letting them go, allowing them to drift away like clouds. In a way it's a bit like watching a movie. You immerse yourself in the action and as the story unfolds everything becomes clear. If you keep freeze-framing and replaying a scene over and over, you lose any perspective you have and might end up not being able to see beyond the scene you have been obsessing about. But if we notice we are doing this, we can say to ourselves, *Ah, hang on. This is the bit where I keep rewinding and ruining the rest of the film.* And then we can move past that.

(Oh, and by the way, the tour of *Sister Act* was a success, a joyous, challenging, exciting experience, because whenever a moment of doubt did creep in, I saw it as a cue that I needed to slow down and listen for my inner wisdom to remind me that I didn't need to pay attention to that internal chatter.)

I understand now that making huge decisions in the middle of a thought storm is ridiculous, and yet this is something that's played out regularly in most relationships (and in life). It's often not about our circumstances, but our thoughts around those circumstances. We get wrapped up with the content of them when we could avoid the whole drama if we just took a step back and observed, realised, *Ahh yes, I'm really pissed off, so this is the time I should not take my thoughts seriously or act on them.* Knowing this helps you step out of the drama. It's good to ask the question: who is in charge? Me or my thoughts? Lemons.

With regard to the lemons, see what happens? We get trapped by them. Trying to control the thought is the problem. I must not think of lemons. I must not think of lemons... Oh God, I'm thinking about lemons. So what can we do instead? We can just think, ah, there's a lemon in my head. Okay, I won't stress about it, I'll accept that it's there, but it won't be for long because another thought will come along and take its place. In this way you take the power away from the thought. Our problems are so often caused by giving too much power to our thoughts – when the reality is that thoughts are like buses, so another one will come along soon (or three at once). We need to trust the process and just wait for the next bus.

While the tumultuous overthinking began when I was very young, it is only now, decades down the line, that I've come to understand how it has affected me. Aha – that's why I play-acted my way through school, trying to pretend I wasn't scared about not belonging. That's why I spent too much time trying to be part of the 'right' group – out of fear. That's why I didn't – couldn't – explore the things that interested me, because I felt I had to fit in with everyone else and that was the only thing that mattered.

I recognise now that I had created a belief system that I didn't belong, and it became so entrenched that it took over my life – so all my efforts were poured into becoming a part of something, and I would do anything and everything to fit the mould. I changed my accent. I changed the way I looked. I convinced people I believed this, that or the other. It was exhausting and it didn't leave me any time or energy to figure out what I actually did believe, what I did like or want. Drama is my passion – but it took a long time to discover that, because at school I played up and pissed about, or skived and avoided it like the plague because it just wasn't 'cool'. Again, as long as I was with the 'right' people, I felt safe and nothing else mattered.

Every one of us has dark or difficult periods, and for me that constant feeling of not belonging, of being other, of not being good enough, which had plagued my childhood and continued well into middle age, caused so many issues that I eventually reached a point where I felt I was unable to help myself and was probably not that much use to those around me either. It impacted my relationship with Brian and he found it very hard to understand how one minute I would be affectionate and the next totally flighty. We ended up hurting each other badly. It made me realise that I couldn't carry on the way I had been, and a personal crisis that saw me hit the wall was the final straw: something had to give.

That's why, in my mid-forties, I decided to try therapy. It was a big decision for me, but I wanted to understand myself and the choices I had made, to get to know me, and to really try to find some peace at last. Sure, I was a fine, functioning human being – on the whole – but there were aspects of my life that I knew I was avoiding yet really needed to deal with to move on to the happier and healthier future I craved. Not least, I had reached a place which scared me, made me realise that this was not how I wanted the next part of my life to go. At one point it got so bad it stopped me in my tracks. Where could I go from there? I knew I had to take action, but I didn't know where to start without getting help.

For someone who has spent a lifetime bottling everything up inside, who has kept all her inner workings secret from even her nearest and dearest – and herself! – the therapist's chair can be daunting, to say the least. The very reason you are there is to open up, to talk about the way you are feeling, and that was something I had absolutely no idea how to do. It took me months to even be able to make eye contact. There were lots and lots of tears; it was very tough.

I didn't really know what to expect from it and I think I was pretty naïve. I thought I'd turn up, they'd fix me and it would all start falling into place in the first session – but of course that wasn't the case at all. As Bob – my then therapist, now friend – likes to say, therapy is a process, not an event. When I first turned up, I was looking for the event, I wanted a quick fix. But then that was the case with everything in my life – it was all about quick fixes for me. I'll do this. That doesn't work, fuck that. I'll try this, fuck that. I was always the master of quick fixes. Always.

So why did I stick this out rather than moving on to the next thing as I always had before? I guess because I was in crisis and I couldn't come up with any other option. And because it was already starting to make me think about things in a very different way. Not that I found that easy. If Bob ever said anything along the lines of, 'Oh, it must have been so difficult for you when your parents did or didn't do this or that,' or, 'That must have been such an awful thing for you to go through,' I would get so defensive: 'Don't you dare say anything about my parents, they're perfect.' I was constantly defending everybody but myself. I felt as though I was betraying my family by saying everything wasn't perfect when they'd always done their best. There was a huge sense of betrayal, and I would get incredibly emotional about things; I just didn't feel comfortable. It was so hard to make myself vulnerable and it was almost like I was looking for a way to escape those conversations. And yet despite all that, it started to make a difference.

I found the theoretical model and practical application of the transactional analysis model (or PAC) really helped me to understand how the psyche works and what we are made up of. While this is obviously not the place for a deep dive into the ins and outs of what are known as our ego states, one might describe our patterns of behaviour in very simple terms like this.

- P = parent. The parent part is split into two sections, the critical parent and the nurturing parent.
- A = adult. The adult bit of us is the one which responds appropriately to given situations, almost like the computer part of you, if you like.
- C = child. This part of us is also made up of two halves, the rebellious (or free) child and the adaptive child.

The adaptive child is all the things that you have learned to use and do to survive within your family. The rebellious – or free – child does what it says on the tin. It can be characterised by defiance, impulsiveness, a desire for independence. My personality was very much dominated by a huge critical parent ego state along with a strong rebellious child, as well as that adaptive child that always tried to fit in. There were too many times I had exhibited risky behaviours in the sense of drinking too much or behaving inappropriately – my rebellious child in action – which would then trigger the critical parent that would admonish me, and the negative spiral would continue from there. The work we were doing in the sessions was all about trying to quieten that critical parent and strengthen the nurturing, empowering parent within my psyche, to begin that shift so that things would – could – start to change. And slowly but surely it did. I learned to let the walls down and began to transform my relationships with myself and those around me. And it wasn't one seismic event, it was a process that slowly allowed the changes to happen and the beliefs about myself to change.

Bob kind of became a parental figure modelled on the nurturing parent ego state. The one that celebrated me. I was not very good at accepting what are known in transactional analysis as strokes (aka compliments). So if someone said, 'Your hair looks amazing today,' my instant response would be, 'Oh God no, it needs washing, it's a mess.' I was never able to accept a compliment and he picked me up on it. It all helped. That said, I realise that therapy in itself is an expense many people cannot afford. Nor would I ever want anyone to think that therapy has all the answers and that it's the only way to go. It's not – honest! But through my experience and further explorations, I have gained lots of insights that I find hugely helpful in my everyday life and have come across many interesting theories. For example, who knew that if there are personalities you really clash with, that you really don't like, that irritate the hell out of you, it's usually because there's something in them that you recognise in yourself? Turns out it's a good thing to test out why they are making you feel that way, and what is it about that person that really grinds your guts, because through this you'll find that thing you recognise and struggle with yourself. It's a really good way to start working on yourself. I've applied this principle to myself and it's helped no end.

People's memories of events can differ. We need only look at eyewitness accounts to crimes to see that they can differ enormously – not because people are lying but because memory is fragile. You have to sometimes question what you believe to be true against other people's truths. In short, we all have our own perspectives on things – and that fascinates me too. Because whenever we're being hard on ourselves, or we make assumptions about what other people are thinking about us, we have to remember again that these thoughts are not necessarily true. This plays so heavily into how women view themselves and their value in relationships. It's been really exciting to use what I've learned and apply it to examples from my own life as well as the universals of being an older woman.

Therapy is not for everyone – for a host of different reasons – but there are many other types of help you can give yourself which are just as valid, things that are accessible to everyone and have free resources. On which note, there will also be a list of resources I've found helpful at the back of the book (page 219), with ideas for websites to visit, articles and books to read, people to find out more about, and so on, so you can find something that resonates with you.

I realise now that my own route to where I am today has been somewhat circuitous at times. There are loads of things that I've done to get to this point and it's only now I've realised, God, I didn't actually need to do all of that at all. It's really fucking simple. I could have just got here by having that 'aha' moment. But then, maybe it's only because of the things I have done that I can think that. Any which way, it's all part of the journey!

Therapy certainly got me thinking in a different way, something that I found illuminating and which I really enjoyed – and which made me realise I wanted to find out more. It also helped me discover enough of a sense of self to be able to explore all this further.

I have always been fascinated by others – yes, I'm nosy – so in some ways I think it was a natural progression for me to study psychotherapy and understand the process more deeply. I even considered becoming a practising therapist myself, though ultimately it was less about wanting to change career than being interested in getting under the bonnet of life. But along with that came something I had in no way foreseen. The deeper I got into it all, the louder my own analytical voice became, and the overthinking started to take over once again. And once again, I didn't recognise this at the time, though I noticed my old patterns coming to the surface and I wasn't enjoying my third year of study as much. I thought this was because I had taken on too much, as I was also grappling with a serial killer in my day job. But in hindsight, I realised I was using my analytical thinking to examine theory to the point that I was overthinking even more, which also meant each question gave rise to another question. So in some ways it simply created a whole new set of issues and ultimately it didn't really solve the problems that I had in the first place. When I felt like I'd 'fixed' one part of myself, I found another area that needed attention. At the end of the day, it felt a bit like peeling an onion: there was always going to be another layer to uncover.

## TIPS

- Don't be afraid to give different things a go. As well as therapy, there are many other options out there, from books to classes to websites, including lots of free resources. It's about finding what works for *you*.
- Learn to understand when you are overthinking – and how to press pause to move away from potential thought storms.
- Be open about seeing things differently.
- Do not obsess about lemons.

# 12

## The Three Principles

While therapy has very much been part of my journey, for me it's been a stepping stone rather than a destination. But it has helped me find the discoveries and techniques which have really transformed things in my life and allowed me to get to a better, stronger place. It made me curious and sparked a desire to read and learn. And this in turn led me to the Three Principles, and the teachings of Syd Banks – and that changed everything for me.

It was almost by accident that I discovered what are often known familiarly as the Three Ps, via a friend I'd met on my psychotherapy training course. She had been a brilliant therapist herself before changing direction after she came across the Three Ps – and the more I heard about it, the more fascinated I became.

Whenever I mention the Three Principles to anyone, the first thing they always ask is, 'What is it?' It's a natural question, a good question, but one for which there isn't really a quick and easy answer – or at least not one that would fit neatly into a paragraph (even though the Principles themselves are very simple). In literal terms, the Three Principles is an understanding of how we work as humans through mind, consciousness and thought. It isn't a prescriptive practice, and you certainly don't need to be a university don to understand it. Nor do you have to buy and read endless tomes to get what it's all about. At the most basic level you might say it's about realising that we have the answers within ourselves – we all do – and it's simply about knowing how to tap in to them. But in reality it's far easier to explain how it works through example.

Therapy can imply that you are a problem that needs fixing, and sometimes I don't think that it's so much about solving problems as being conditioned to search for intellectual answers. I thought I was broken but, actually, I wasn't at all. It was simply that my thinking was off. Overthinking – my speciality – can all too easily overtake common sense or intuition. It's a term we often hear or use, while not necessarily considering its true meaning. Overthinking can also override instinct. Instead of going with our gut or finding our own answers inside us, it drowns out our ability to listen out for them. It puts too much emphasis on us constantly trying to problem-solve – but what if there wasn't a problem in the first place?

The Three Principles believes we are all innately well – but our thoughts can fuck up our reality. It focuses on simple and accessible things that we can all explore. It's simply a description of who we are, as humans, and where we fit in this world, the fundamental basis of everything about being human. It's like gravity; you can't see it, but it's there and you can feel the effects of it around you all the time. If you like, it's a description of what we truly are.

I could try to explain the Three Principles until the cows come home but will resist that here, and instead will offer suggestions for further reading later on. But in summary, they are the foundational concepts in understanding human experience and psychological wellbeing.

**Mind:** The first principle refers to the creative power of thought that shapes our subjective experience of reality. According to Syd Banks, the philosopher behind the Three Principles, the mind is the source of all human experience. It's often easier to explain using analogy, so perhaps think of it as a projector that generates our thoughts, feelings and perceptions, creating our inner world and shaping our external reality.

**Consciousness:** The second principle refers to our capacity for awareness – or consciousness. This is what allows us to be aware of our thoughts, emotions and experiences. Consciousness is our innate ability to be aware of what's happening in the present moment, without judgement, distraction or analysis.

**Thought:** The third principle refers to the transient and ever-changing nature of thought. Thoughts arise spontaneously in our minds and continually flow through our consciousness. They are the medium through which we experience life and interpret reality. Banks emphasises the fact that thoughts are not inherently good or bad; they're simply the natural by-product of the creative power of the mind.

He believes that understanding these principles can lead to greater psychological resilience, clarity and wellbeing, as we realise our innate capacity to navigate life's challenges and create positive change from within.

You could say that the crux of it is about understanding that every feeling and emotion is created by your own thoughts, and the realisation that those thoughts are not facts. Getting caught up in horrible or distressing thoughts will lead us to experience pain, but there is a way to avoid this. By becoming aware of thought patterns, we can choose to challenge them. We can look for evidence that supports or contradicts the negative thinking, which is very often based on assumptions rather than reality in the first place.

It's all too easy to get bound up in bad memories, but these are just thoughts about things that have happened in the past, and which are creating those feelings. When we become aware of this, those thoughts lose their power to impact us.

There is always another way of looking at yourself. The stories that we tell ourselves (there's something wrong with me... I'm not good enough... if people knew what I was really like, they wouldn't like me) are just beliefs we choose to buy into, and when you recognise your low-mood thinking, you can take action. Understand that we create our insecure thinking; we live the stories we've created about ourselves. Take the thing I've had running through my life about not belonging, being other. It's taken until this point to realise, *Oh my God, I always fucking belonged*. But that's exactly my point; that was all in my thinking. I told myself I didn't belong. Nobody actually said it to me; I created that belief myself. So it's about understanding how thoughts work, and that just because you think something doesn't mean it's true. The fact is that you can look externally to belong and feel like you do until somebody utters one sentence and then you feel like you don't belong at all. And yet we all belong. Belonging comes down to love and compassion for yourself, valuing and seeing yourself for who you really are, and not that you are there to fit in.

Ninety-seven per cent of people in any room will feel like they don't belong. It's a universal feeling. But we belong by default. The second we were born we belonged.

If we tell ourselves, 'I must do better,' 'I should feel this,' 'If I just do this, then…' it simply takes us in the wrong direction. When we are experiencing love and compassion it comes from a place of non-judgement and it feels amazing. How do we find it? We listen for it. It's accessible to us all. We don't have to search outside. It's in us, available to us all the time. The psychologist Dicken Bettinger calls it our drop-in centre. It's open all hours and the only thing that's banned in there is judgement. When you become aware of your overthinking and realise that you need to step out of your thoughts, then you can enter this space to find what you need. I can visualise my space, and it brings me back into the present. It took me a while to find it, but once I did, it changed so much.

When you're having a really good time or when you're in a really happy place, you just get on and enjoy it. You don't question it. But when you're in a bad place, you find yourself spiralling into a barrage of thoughts. What's wrong with me? Why did they do that? Why has that happened? We question everything. We don't just say 'shit happens' and move on. There's a great saying by American psychotherapist, Richard Carlson: 'The trick is to be grateful when your mood is high, and graceful when it is low.'* I always love that. And it's so very true; when we participate in things that make us happy and fulfilled, when we are doing the things we love, we tend to be in the present

*Richard Carlson, *Don't Worry, Make Money: Spiritual and Practical Ways to Create Abundance and More Fun in Your Life* (Hearst Publications, 1997).

rather than bound up in our thoughts and memories. Of course, we will all experience negative feelings – that is part of being human. But it's how we deal with them that makes all the difference.

Like anyone else, I get loads of insecure thoughts, but I've now reached a place where I understand that my thinking does not always equal the truth. And now I'm aware of it (mostly, but definitely not always. Still a work in progress) – and can sometimes even laugh about it – I've found it has really helped me not to take my thoughts personally and allow them to bring me down.

This is something we have to do for ourselves. It's important to remember that we can't change anyone else, but we can change what's in our own minds. Only we are in control of what we believe.

My life changed simply because my thinking changed. I stopped overthinking. I chose not to listen to that tired old voice that said, 'Stay under the radar. Be grateful. Know your limitations.' I gave up my beliefs about myself and I started to realise that my thinking was distorting my real life and there were steps I could take to change that.

Compelling thoughts happen when you're most upset. Impulsivity happens a lot when you're in a low mood. It's taken me most of my adult life to get to see that. When I look back at some of the things I got wrong and some of the bad decisions I made in the past, I can now see that they came from when I was in a low place. That's an incredibly rewarding insight and it's through that that I have learned to forgive myself. When you realise that you were wrong, you can be accountable, and you can stop. Just remember that the more you think about something, the more real it gets. We create so much pain and suffering from the things we tell ourselves.

The only experience we need to understand human nature is to be human. Wisdom is something every single one of us is born with. It is simple enough, but do we always pay attention to our own wisdom? We do not. We get caught up in intellect, which is something very different. Intellect is learned, whether it's from books or libraries, courses, exams and appraisals, studying, testing, experimenting. Wisdom is so quiet and so gentle it can brush us like a feather – so lightly that we may miss it. But it's there, and every one of us has experienced it. That little voice that says, 'Maybe it would be better not to say what I'm currently thinking' (though we often blurt it out anyway and hurt someone in the process – and then wish we hadn't). The one that got me to hold back when I wanted to lamp the health visitor who made that comment about being geriatric.

These learnings have absolutely changed my life. They don't make me perfect. They don't stop bad things happening (I'm human – we all have shitty times) or negative feelings creeping in. But they have given me an awareness that we can find a way through difficult periods. When something has got me down, I am able to take a step back and think, *This is not okay*. Instead of getting myself in a state about it or kicking back and rebelling, which was my answer for so many years, I have learned to have a quick seethe and then tune in to that little voice which is reminding me that I have a really low level of self-awareness at that point. It helps me to acknowledge what I'm feeling and stop ruminating about it all, to just notice it then let it go, and get on with the day without letting it take up any more space in my brain, knowing that by the next day, it's gone. It can just give you a bit of comfort and make things a little bit easier.

It's only natural to have times when we fixate on perceived problems or future scenarios, or we become convinced that something terrible is about to happen. But if you can just catch yourself doing this, you can separate thought from reality and that makes it so much easier to deal with. And that is exactly the point of it all. It is this understanding that has turned my life around.

Syd Banks says that it is only in our head that tomorrow and yesterday exist, and it's so true that we often attach so much to what's gone and what's to come. We only have now. I was reminded of this not long ago when I was in Lapland as patron of the charity When You Wish Upon a Star. After a very exciting day we were heading back to the airport, but before that we spent the last hour of the trip at Santa's village. To be honest, it's a bit like a Christmassy version of Cheshire Oaks shopping village, but I thought I'd rush into the shops, as they were about to close, and pick up some decorations, a souvenir, a bauble, so that every time I looked at it, I could remember that time I was in Lapland with the kids. As a result of this I missed the most spectacular display of the Earth's greatest light show: the aurora borealis or northern lights. By planning for the future, I had missed the experience in the present. We need to bear witness, become aware, ground ourselves. To stop multitasking all the time and focus on the job in hand.

We all have those moments where we say 'I lost track of time' because we have been so wrapped up in what we are doing. These are often attached to good experiences in our lives; there is truth in the adage that time flies when we are having fun. But our minds will naturally wander. It's lovely to reminisce and it's lovely to fantasise about things coming up, but we need to do it with awareness. Looking backwards can be painful. The past is done, finished with. We can't change anything. Yes, it's useful to help us to learn lessons, but if we find ourselves going over and over something that has happened, it can be destructive. Anticipating the future can also be great if there is something we are excited about or looking forwards to, but, ultimately, things are very unlikely to match the rehearsed version in our heads and so we are in danger of setting ourselves up for disappointment. I've mentioned before that sometimes I struggled to be 'present', and like so many of us, got caught up in things that had happened in the past, which were not always good things, or spent too much time trying to look ahead into the future, which sometimes evoked anxiety and fear. That's all perfectly normal, of course. It's a very human trait, and it's not realistic to be in the present at all times. There will always be times when we want to enjoy certain memories, or look forward to future plans. But it's important not to get too caught up in that, or it will mean that you often miss the moment by taking yourself away from the present and what's happening around you in the here and now.

One of the ways I would often find myself looking ahead rather than living in the moment was when it came to holidays. I would find myself longing for the times of the year I'd get to travel. Visiting different countries, exploring different cultures is something I will never tire of, but the more I got into the Three Principles, the more I realised that I was spending way too much time projecting into the future. I'd say things like, 'Oh I can't wait for my trip...', 'It's only five weeks until we...', 'Roll on April...' Of course, it's pleasurable to have nice things to look forward to, but we need to be careful that it doesn't drag us out of living in the present too much. I misunderstood. I thought travelling took me to my happy place. Helped me to switch off. I missed the point that I could access my happy place or switch off any time I wanted. All those good feelings were already within me if I quietened down my thinking and immersed myself in the life I was living moment to moment.

We spend a lot of our time forward thinking, applying strategies, being goal-oriented, planning our retirements. I accept that it's prudent for us to save for a rainy day – but there is not a single human on the planet who can predict the future. Also, the future we are planning is governed by the thoughts and feelings we have *today*. And as it says on the cover – we are all works in progress, constantly evolving and changing. My friend Sarie, a Three Principles practitioner, came up with this great analogy. Imagine asking your eleven-year-old self who you should be living with, what job you should be doing and where you should be living in ten years' time. I rest my case.

If we are feeling insecure in ourselves, or inadequate, we will only be able to see a self-limiting future based on what we have believed until now. It's so important we trust ourselves more. All we have to do is show up and realise we only have right now. The only thing that is guaranteed in life is change. It is our choice to be scared by it or to embrace it and think how incredible it is that we can experience something new from moment to moment. When we are present, we listen to ourselves, we prioritise ourselves, we don't compare ourselves to others. We are able to be our true self.

We do need to create space from our thinking. When we switch off, we reset. Being present doesn't mean being quiet. It has nothing to do with outside circumstances. We can be present amid chaos. We can get present whilst shopping at Tesco. We just need to make time to step back from the noise, or our past and future thoughts.

People use all sorts of techniques to ground themselves – such as yoga or meditation – and if you enjoy it, great, carry on. Personally, I don't, because at some point you have to stop the act of meditation, or the yoga class ends. I don't think you need to do anything. For me it's just a little internal voice, if you like, just three words when I find myself ruminating, worrying or stressing. *Let it go.* Of course I don't manage it all the time; I'm human, so it's my job to get it wrong. But there are plenty of times when I do catch myself, and in doing so save myself a lot of unpleasant and fretful thinking.

Anxiety lives in our future thoughts. Some of my own most anxious moments used to be around sleep and whether I was getting enough of it. I would get frantic if I was awake at 2 a.m.; my thoughts would become louder and louder. *Oh God, I can't sleep. I have to sleep. How am I going to get through tomorrow if I don't sleep? I'm going to be so tired and I've got ten scenes to film. I won't make it through the day; there's no way I will remember my lines.* (Is it any wonder that you then can't get back to sleep?!) I had always assumed that these thoughts were reality, when the *actual* reality was that I always made it through the day whether I had slept well or not. I always remembered my lines, but I don't ever recall a time during the day when I said to myself, *I must remember that I'm really tired and I'm not going to make it through, and I need to remember that I don't know my lines*. It was always fine. In the wee hours of the morning, though, when my state of consciousness was low, I truly believed that being awake at 2 a.m. would destroy the next day completely. It never did. I might have felt tired, but so what?

Nowadays when I wake at 2 a.m., I am much more likely to catch my thoughts and to recognise them for what they are. Just thoughts. I smile at them. *Oh, here we go, this is the bit where I start living in the future and catastrophising about the next day*. Just doing this is often enough to allow me to scan my body, starting at my head and relaxing all the way down to the tips of my toes, or to take my oft-nightly flight on the back of an eagle, where we fly up the side of Everest, observe the queue to reach the summit, exchange glances with a large yeti, swoop over a snow leopard sitting on a rock, licking its paw. We then quite quickly dip over an Austrian alpine meadow (very *Sound of Music)* to a rather nice Bavarian-style house with a couple of cows and a river that meanders through various landscapes, which then somehow becomes a beach in the Maldives with obligatory dolphins, a few puffins (I know I'm in the wrong continent for puffins but hey, it's my dream), and then I'm woken by the alarm. If those bad thoughts persist, I just notice them and their power over me eases. I replace them with more pleasant ones instead.

Our minds are constantly wandering. While standing in a queue at the checkout we might go word for word through the argument we are going to have (or more likely that we are never going to have!) with a person who's annoyed us. We imagine we are actually having that argument, what they're saying or thinking back. In the same way we fantasise about future scenarios and events, real or otherwise. We might see ourselves living out our fantasy jobs or lying on a tropical beach. We might ask what will happen when we meet someone we haven't seen for years. And in this way we can lose large parts of our days; in fact, a Harvard study suggests we spend as much as 47 per cent of our waking hours daydreaming.* This is done unconsciously by all of us, and constantly rehearsing how things are going to go or play out is all very well for daytime, but when those thoughts shift to unhelpful nightmares, it's good to be able to stop them in their tracks. I know I can sound like a stuck record, but again, everything comes back to being aware.

We use energy to create images and then we choose which ones we give life to and which ones just to let disappear like a puff of smoke. We might see a group of kids playing outside in the street and think, *Ahh, look at them, just enjoying the sunshine and having fun. It's so nice to stand and watch them out of the window*. Or we might see a group of kids playing outside in the street and think, *If those little shits don't shut the fuck up, I swear to God I am going to lose my shit*. Our reaction has nothing to do with the kids but is about our state of consciousness at that moment and the thoughts it brings up.

How come some people can live right next to a railway line or dual carriageway? Because their thinking is not wrapped up with the sound. They still hear the sound, but it's not something they give time and thought to. They probably noticed it when they first moved in, but I bet if you knocked on the door and asked them about it, they would say, 'It's not something we really think about.'

*Matthew Killingsworth and Daniel Gilbert, 'A Wandering Mind is an Unhappy Mind', *Science*, vol. 330, Issue 6006, 12 November 2010, p. 932.

One of the reasons I'm such a fan of the Three Principles is because it uses the wisdom we all have within ourselves to keep our thoughts from consuming us. There are many forms of help or therapy that people use to work on their beliefs or solve problems or issues in relationships and so on, but as long as we are searching for what's wrong with us, what faults we have, asking ourselves, 'Why am I such a bad person?' and so on, all it does is remind us that we are wrapped up in thinking about our thinking. It can be like trying to change the picture after you've already painted it.

The Three Principles is absolutely *not* about positive thinking; God no, that's exhausting. *I must be positive. I must think positive thoughts*... Does positive thinking help an addict? No, quite the opposite. Mental health is not about being positive. Shit happens. People get ill, accidents happen, people die. Relationships break down. When we overthink, we get stuck in time, and we just regurgitate all that thinking. Becoming aware and understanding how thought works is key and provides comfort.

Self-help manuals often tell us that we need a toolbox for life. No – we don't need toolboxes. Again, this implies that we need fixing! Dr Judy Sedgeman, another leading Three Principles practitioner, says the only tool any of us have is the ability to think. People come up with so many ways, techniques or modalities to help, but as she also says, if you go to 450 therapists, you will get 450 treatment plans.

The feelings I struggled with didn't just suddenly disappear, and even now they linger at the edges. But at last I have learned how to keep them there rather than letting them take over. It's taken time, effort and the ability to find or create some quiet moments to work my way through everything – and to finally realise that overthinking was not my friend and was not benefiting me in any way whatsoever. The feelings have gone, in the sense that I am at peace with myself 75 per cent of the time. I don't pay much attention to what others think of me. Only people who are in my life really know me. I like myself a lot more of the time than I dislike myself. Whether that's a C or a B+, whatever it is, I've passed.

## TIPS

- **Write down whatever it is that is worrying you as it is happening.** I will stick it down on paper with the intention of coming back to it later in the day to address it – but quite often I forget to come back to it, because my level of consciousness has changed or I'm in a different mood and the worry has become insignificant. Also, postponing the anxious thought helped me break the habit of overthinking the situation. I won't try to quieten or ignore my anxious thoughts, but I just make the decision to address them at a later point in the day, say at 4 p.m. That act in itself means I can park them and move on to the things I need to be getting on with rather than not being able to focus on those because my mind is already full of stress.
- **Stop seeing things as black and white.** It's too easy to think of things in this way (*It's all their fault. They did this, they did that, it's all down to them.*), when usually there is nuance involved and we have played our own part in the situation, often without

realising. Once you appreciate and explore, then it's often much easier to understand a situation and therefore what you can do about it.

- **Notice your habits.** Do you have a tendency to emphasise the bad and diminish the good? Becoming aware of it will help you avoid it in future.
- **Ask yourself whether your thought is helpful.** If it's not constructive, then move on.
- **Start to listen to your own wisdom.** Trust your instincts, and if it's loud and noisy and doesn't feel good, it's not wisdom.
- **What would I say to a friend if they came to me with this?** It always seems so much easier to solve or help with other people's thoughts, worries or problems than our own. Asking yourself this question allows you to bring a different perspective, and sometimes that detachment can really make a difference.

# 13

## Breaking the Patterns

I'll have another drink – it won't hurt just this once…

You do something because you enjoy it, it brings pleasure or it feels like it fulfils a need at that particular time. It stops the overthinking for a bit. So you do it again. And again. At some point down the line, you decide that you want to stop… then discover it's just not that easy. It's become addictive, a pattern of behaviour that feels difficult, even impossible, to break. Sound familiar? It's something I know about all too well.

My relationship with alcohol started a long time ago. There were student parties, of course, and the usual nights out you have in your late teens and early twenties (which often ended up with being reacquainted with whatever I'd had for dinner a few hours earlier – put me off diced carrots for years). But I started to see drinking differently when I met Michael and Lesley. That was my introduction to the world of sophisticated dining and bonhomie. It was a whole new world, as drinking had never been a thing in my family. My parents very rarely had a drink. They had a cupboard full of alcohol which they had been given as end-of-term presents, and there was a bottle of wine that probably stayed in there for about seven years. I know this because I nicked it and took it to the playground and tried to drink it with my mates, and it was like vinegar. But no, they weren't drinkers. My grandma liked a cider on Christmas Day, and I'd maybe get a sip or the odd taste of shandy, but that was it. Michael and Lesley were so much more worldly and part of an acting culture where things were very different from what I was used to. It was like everything was an event or a celebration – the end of a performance was reason enough – and at Sunday lunch, out would come the wine, and I was like, *Oh my God, this is so cultured. This is what we do now, we have wine with our dinner. I mean, get me*. I felt like a proper grown-up and I loved it.

When I started working in TV, where everyone around me was at it, I saw no reason not to carry on drinking. In our industry you were almost expected to drink; it was as though deals were done with a glass in hand and important meetings would take place over a boozy lunch. At the end of a filming day you would head to the pub, the BBC bar, or the one at Granada Studios, the Old School. They were always packed every single lunchtime with staff, and certain stars could always be found propping up the bar, worse for wear, only to venture back onto set stinking of booze. It's extraordinary to me that this was overlooked for so many years. Lighting riggers responsible for securing lights directly above people's heads, directors responsible for overseeing the filming… this was the norm across the TV industry, which was still very traditional in its style of doing business. At the time, I don't think any of us thought too much of it, but actually these were shocking standards which have now been witnessed in many of the unsavoury revelations about some major household names.

The pressure to drink, to be part of this booze culture, was immense, and othering yourself could even prove detrimental to your career. A female producer friend, whose male colleagues ended up in the pub every lunchtime and never bothered going back to the office for the rest of the day, noted that they were the ones getting pay rises and promotions, despite the fact that she was the one doing all the work. It's unutterably depressing.

I really loved red wine, but I reached a point where if we were having some, I wouldn't stop at a glass – I'd drink the bottle. And I started drinking more often too. It was almost like I was self-medicating to deal with the stress in my life, and it's often all too easy to drown our sorrows with alcohol (or smother them in chocolate – or whichever substance floats your boat). I don't think I realised that it was becoming a thing, though. It kind of crept up on me and then it became a habit. This was a time when, as a society, it was almost the norm that most weekends half the country would be drinking to excess, so while it wasn't a great habit, there was nothing particularly out of the ordinary about it. It felt almost as though there was an expectation that to enjoy something one needed to have a glass in one's hand (and it was only when I eventually broke the cycle that I realised it was another self-imposed belief that clearly wasn't true). It got to the stage when I was only having two nights off a week, unless I was working on a major storyline and I knew I'd have to be in every day at 7 a.m. – obviously in that situation you can't drink the night before, though I admit there were a couple of occasions when I probably took it too far all the same.

One of them was Ryan Thomas's twenty-first. Ryan played my screen son Jason for almost sixteen years, so we were very close, and that night I ended up partying much harder than I intended to – despite knowing I had a very early start. In fact, it made total sense to me to head straight from the party – at two in the morning – to the studios nearby and sneak into my dressing room and sleep until my make-up call. Thankfully no one was any the wiser and I definitely wasn't the only person to do this over the years. I admit too that some of my best lunchtime snoozes have been on a well-known character's bed on set. This definitely wouldn't be possible today, but back in the good old Granada TV days it wasn't something we really thought twice about.

Drinking seemed like a good way to relax, or to feel like one of the gang, or to take me away from myself for a while, but in reality it didn't benefit me in any way – quite the opposite. There was the entire night I spent talking to acting legend Peter O'Toole, trying to match him drink for drink. I was aware at the time this was a real once-in-a-lifetime opportunity and a chance to hear some of the most incredible stories. Unfortunately I got so pissed I couldn't remember a single one afterwards.

There was also the time I was filming with comedian and actor Harry Enfield, and one of the sketches required us to use a whole load of fake money. The banknotes were so realistic that they had to give them special serial numbers logged to the production so that they didn't get used in real life. Harry and I both had young kids, so we nabbed a few afterwards for them to use in their toy tills. On my way home, I ended up at Soho House, a members' club in central London, where there was a lot of drinking. When it was my turn to buy a round, I told someone to grab some cash out of my bag. It was only the next day when

I tried to find the money for Elliot's till that I realised it was no longer there. You can guess what had happened. That was the point that I realised that I had also given fellow actress Gwyneth Strong a fake £20 for a taxi home. That was funny at the time, but looking back, it wasn't exactly a career highlight.

I got used to drinking. It became my norm and once I'd had a taste of it, that was it. I'm a glugger not a sipper, so taking it slowly was not an option. I always said I'd be much better if I drank pints, but I didn't like the taste of beer, I didn't like shorts, and I didn't like anything else. I just loved red wine. So I would drink too much of it and it kind of crept up on me insidiously. It went from weekends to four or five nights a week. This was when Elliott was quite small, the time when my marriage wasn't going well and I felt I had lost all my creativity, and I lost myself. Some nights James and I would share a bottle of wine over dinner and then, other nights, I'd just have the whole bottle to myself. If James didn't want any, I'd open it anyway. I'd have a glass while I was cooking, a couple of glasses with dinner and then, when it was time for bed, there'd be a little bit left, and I'd think, *What's the point of keeping that?* so I'd finish it off just because.

I think booze played its part in dulling the effects of menopause too, although I didn't think of it like that at the time, and it's only with hindsight that I can see that I was using the wine to deal with some of the symptoms. I carried on having periods until very, very late. I was still having them every month until I was fifty-eight. I didn't get any hot flushes or anything like that, but I had weird sensations. Like when I was driving, I'd get this sort of tunnel vision – as though the car was still and everything else was moving.

I went to a friend and said, 'Oh my God, I think I've got a brain tumour or something' (you have to bear in mind that I'm quite dramatic and then factor in a bit of hypochondria as well). It was Sally Dynevor who plays Sally Metcalfe in *Coronation Street*, and she said, 'You know that it could be the menopause?' She recommended a hormone doctor, this amazing endocrinologist called Annice Mukherjee, so I went to see her, and although it's a fairly unusual symptom, she had heard of it before. I told her I was also feeling a bit flat. Nothing I could put my finger on, just flat. So she started me on hormone replacement therapy (HRT) and it made such a difference. That said, I'm very aware that HRT isn't for everyone; there are some people who can't take it for medical and other reasons, and for those who can, it certainly isn't one size fits all. But what I would say is that if you're struggling, it's worth seeking help.

All the same, eventually I reached a stage when I knew I was drinking too much and that it was not healthy. I'd find myself saying in the mornings, 'I promise that tonight I won't' – but somehow I always did. Over the pandemic it kept on creeping up and up (and I kept piling on the pounds), and I suddenly realised that on the nights I didn't drink, I missed it. This was when I understood that alcohol had become a habit – I had become a habitual drinker – and it was time to do something about it.

As with anything, there are different ways to address addictive behaviours, depending on personality, circumstances and more. For me? I'm very much an all-or-nothing sort of person and I need to do things my way. I used to smoke years ago, and once I made up my mind to give up, that was it. I didn't tell anyone I was doing it. I stopped at midnight one New Year's Eve, and it was only about three weeks later that Brian and Elliott said, 'Hang on, you've not had a cigarette for ages.' I was like, 'Yes, I decided to stop but I didn't tell you because I didn't want any outside pressure.' I guess it's that rebellious streak of mine: if anyone says anything to me, I will simply push against it, even going against or hurting myself in order to do that, simply to not conform. I was worried that if someone said anything I'd just turn round and say, 'Fuck you,' and have one just to spite them. So that's what I did with the drink too.

The thing about me is that if I can spark an interest and think 'I wonder if…', if I can become curious about something, I find that's when change really happens. 'I wonder what it would be like? I wonder why I love alcohol so much, why do I look forward to it so much? Why does the thought of an evening without red wine fill me with dread?' So I went online and found Annie Grace's alcohol experiment,* which is thirty days of giving up alcohol and learning about what alcohol does. Deep-down stuff you probably already know, but a useful refresher nonetheless. The programme also taps in to how you feel. I figured I'd do that for January, but it became like a lightbulb moment for me. I went back to drinking for a couple of weeks before saying to Brian, 'You know, I might just stop for another month.' And I just didn't go back to drinking at all.

I learned from Annie Grace's course that there are three main types of alcohol: isopropanol, which is found in hand sanitisers, paint thinners, household cleaners; methanol, which is used for fuelling cars and ships and for making household products; and ethanol, which is found in

*thisnakedmind.com/annie-grace/ Annie Grace is also the author of several books, including *The Alcohol Experiment.*

lotions, paints and cleansing products. All of these have the ability to kill us, and yet we choose to consume ethanol in alcoholic drinks. Alcohol is an addictive substance; if you drink, you inevitably sit somewhere on the spectrum of it potentially being a problem. But the problem is not you, it's the substance itself. If you want to take a look at alcohol and its effects, I urge you to take a close look at Annie Grace's alcohol experiment. She opened my eyes to seeing drinking in a different way.

There have been a couple of times when I have thought I might have a glass. For me it's never been a case of 'I'm never going to drink again'. I just wanted to have a break and to stop that pandemic habit in its tracks. When you come out of the jungle and cross the bridge on *I'm a Celebrity*, Ant and Dec have a glass of champagne there waiting for you, so I thought I might have a drink then – but in the end, I decided not to have it. Then I thought I might have a glass on Christmas Day, but it came and went. I tried to have a glass of champagne on holiday, but just one sip made me feel like I was thirteen again, where you have to force yourself to swallow it. And now here I am.

But like I say, never say never, because one day I might decide to have one, though I'm not sure it will happen. Because the minute I make it about self-control it becomes about conforming again and that's something I can't do. If anything for me is about self-discipline rather than free choice, forget it, because there's always an end point to that, and it's not in my psyche. I've just made a decision that right now I don't want to drink because it's not benefiting me, but I'm not trying to prove anything to anyone.

I stopped by not putting pressure on myself. In the past I might have decided to have thirty days off alcohol but then believed I had messed up if I ended up drinking on one or two. I'd call myself a failure and end up opening a bottle as a 'fuck it, I'm useless' kind of salve. Annie Grace showed me that if you slipped up for two days out of thirty then it was still a 93 per cent success rate. That's amazing – and the perfect way to change your mindset.

We are bombarded every day by adverts for alcoholic drinks on TV, on the sides of buses, in magazines. We now know it does as much damage to the human body as smoking – and yet most celebrations are centred around it. It's the norm for birthdays, funerals, Christmas, weddings, parties, pubs, clubs – family occasions of every shape and size. It's no longer acceptable to smoke at these events, for obvious reasons, and yet we are reluctant to admit that alcohol is a similarly toxic substance. We believe our stories around alcohol. It's like I believed that I couldn't enjoy social events and parties without a drink in my hand. That was the story I told myself, but the reality is that if you drink in the midst of something that is already fun, you are teaching your subconscious that it was the drinking that was fun. I believed I couldn't sleep well unless I had a drink. The reality is I never fall asleep in the day any more and now the quality of my sleep is incredible.

One wise thought has the power to change your life, but most of the time we just don't listen. Yet when we do, we are capable of massive changes – thanks to a minuscule trillion-millionth-of-a-second bit of wisdom that pops into our head. We spend so much time going round in circles with our thoughts that we can be blind to that moment where something so powerful drops, it can alter the course of your life. It isn't just another thought – it comes from somewhere deeper. It's quiet, it's soft, it's not judgemental.

It just nudges you. It's a feeling. For me it was as simple as, *I wonder what it would be like to not drink*, and that one insight was enough to set me on the path of living alcohol-free. And I feel a million times better for doing it.

Another area where so many women struggle is with food. And yes, this was one that got me too.

I've battled with my body image all my life. I can remember exactly when the whole thing started. I was ten years old, a normal, slim, very tall, long-legged girl – always taller than my friends. The terms 'lanky' or 'bony Maloney' were ones I was used to hearing over and over again. I was just at the age where I'd started to notice fashion and the rage at the time was for Afghan coats and long boots. The trouble was my legs were quite skinny.

I remember trying boots on and the assistant saying, 'Oh, no, you need to wear shoes. These all look like wellies on you. You could get both legs in one boot.' And that's when I started to dislike my shape, the shape of my ankles and calves. By my teens I had a damn fine pair of pins, but could I see that? Absolutely not – because already peer pressure had kicked in and a wisecrack throwaway comment by a Dolcis shop assistant had made me feel shame about my body. Of course, the reality was I had fabulous legs, but that was something I didn't realise or understand back then.

That experience in that shoe shop led my loud, obnoxious internal critic to take form and from that day forward, that critic made itself heard and it felt like it was growing more powerful every day as puberty loomed – and beyond. My body was my enemy and things only got worse. I was frightened of it; age thirteen, I already wanted a different body. I wanted to be curvier, though the lanky, tall body that the boots wouldn't fit seemed not to be a problem for inappropriate older men, who should have known and done better. I hadn't even had my first period when I realised that one of my music teachers' intentions were far more sinister than showing me how to play Vivaldi: I was aware enough it was wrong but didn't have the vocabulary to explain to anyone why I was feeling disgust, unease, anxiety and revulsion. My chosen way of expressing myself was by being difficult, disobeying rules, not practising my instrument, being disruptive. I developed a dislike of men, apart from my dad and my brother.

So how does a young person process these events? By turning inwards. I thought if my legs were bigger, I'd be able to get boots and I'd fit in and be normal. I thought, *If I eat more food, that predator will leave me alone*. Then I started thinking, *I feel better when I eat. It comforts me. It eases the uneasy feelings and it soothes me*. And, of course, there begins the relentless battle in my head: food equals feeling safe. Food equals I'll fit in. Food equals keeping my emotions in check. Food equals a superpower I can use to stop feeling.

This battle continues to be my life's work. I understand a lot more now and that's definitely helped, but it took me until my fifties to start to realise how food served me when I was a young woman, when eating felt like the only solution to my problems. Thankfully I have better resources now, more effective ways of exploring my emotions, and that is far healthier. I was able to stop using food to make myself feel better, just as I stopped drinking far too much red wine, and it made a real difference. When viewers have seen me recently on TV, there's obviously been a change in the way I am and the way I look, and many of the people who've noticed it are – just like me in the past – looking for that magic solution, the diet, the way to live that will transform our lives and rid us for ever of our excess weight. The truth is that I don't believe in those diets: cut carbs, eat for your blood type, the F-Plan, blah, blah, blah... Diets only work when you are prepared to restrict yourself to a way of eating. Willpower is always finite, unless you are an exceedingly driven person who loves order, structure and control – and, obviously, most people are not like that, especially those who need to lose weight. It stands to reason.

So how did I approach it? The short answer is, as I would with any other addictive behaviour... it was all about getting curious. I believe that it's only when you take a true interest in your chosen addiction that things can start to change. Curiosity did not kill the cat! Trust me, as a sixty-year-old woman, I had tried everything and yeah, short-term diets might do the trick, but after that they are simply not sustainable. If you have to get into a Marilyn Monroe dress for the Met Gala, then yes, a crash diet will help lose a bit of timber. But if diets worked in the long term, why do they keep developing new ones every five minutes? It's all bullshit.

Weight issues can, of course, be affected by genetics and hormones and other factors but I believe that mine have, in the main, been for one reason and one reason only: what's been going on in my head. Nothing to do with my glands or my metabolism or my blood type. It was my thoughts which created problems with food, drink, sugar, impulsive behaviours, overthinking, anger, sadness, erratic moments. Those thoughts were perfectly innocent. I just didn't understand at that point that I was the creator of my own experience. Eating, drinking and risky behaviours were all down to me trying to shut out my overthinking, to quieten the thoughts that were so bloody loud.

So what worked for me? Giving up the booze certainly made a big difference to my body shape. So did being in the jungle (which I highly recommend, unless you hate beans or have a phobia about spiders, rats or bugs). So did being ill – more of which later – which I admit I do not recommend at all. Different things work for different people, and being prescriptive is pointless. Being curious, however, can open up a world of opportunities and lead you to changes you never imagined.

The way people treat any form of addiction – be it food, alcohol, or anything else – can often be quite degrading. If you're overweight, you hear, 'You need to be healthy, you need your BMI to be this...' It's all put to us in a very shame-based way. And for me that's a totally unhelpful approach because it just makes me want to eat more (or drink more or smoke more). Nobody chooses to become addicted to something and that's why I get so angry at the diet industry – because it doesn't work. We are still sold this myth when it's far more important to do the work on the inside. Understand the triggers, the hows and the whys, without it all being about denying yourself. So rather than it being *'I need to lose'*, *'I need to stop'*, *'I need to stop eating/drinking'*, *'Oh God, I'm eating/drinking so much'*, *'I can't drink tonight, I mustn't eat such and such tonight,'* it's more about '*I wonder what would happen if...*' Once you start to address those questions, the world opens up.

Sometimes there are medical reasons why losing weight is a good idea. But aside from that, there is far too much pressure to conform to what society tells us we should look like; is it any wonder people feel ashamed that they don't fit? We believe that we have to be a certain way, and the answer is we don't. You are shamed into losing weight in the first place, you're shamed if you struggle, you're even shamed in the way you choose to lose it. But you can only try your best because, at the end of the day, it is an addiction like any other. And as we all know, addictions are not just a case of pulling yourself together. If you have never had an addiction, think yourself fucking lucky. Because I'm sure there are areas of your life where you are following patterns that you find hard to change and which mean you are not doing the best for yourself that you could – and it's the same thing.

But here's the thing – you're told you're taking up too much space, so you try to lose weight. You do a diet, and it doesn't work or you fall off the wagon. More shame. So you try exercise and go to the gym. But you struggle with that and you are hungry all the time. Shame around that too. I hear this from other women all the time. Small wonder that some then put themselves through painful and extreme procedures to try and fix their 'problem' because society doesn't approve of their appearance. And yes, you guessed it, they are shamed for doing so.

It's easy to say, but what other people think really doesn't matter. This is about you: how you feel, what's right for you. The most important thing is to find what resonates with *you*. What works for me may be different from what works for you, but stay curious and the answers will come. I reference all the materials that I've read, learned from and used in my life at the back of this book (page 219). If they are useful for you, that's great. But if not, use them as a jumping-off point and keep looking for the right fit for you – but keep in mind that you should never let your weight define you; you are far more than just a dress size.

In the meantime, it's important to remember that shame rears its head when we believe something about ourselves or something we have been told – for example, the Dolcis assistant's comments about my legs. I'm sure she was simply making light-hearted banter with my mother and was no doubt getting infuriated with my requests to try on every pair of boots available. Maybe she'd looked at my mother's exhausted face after having to traipse through every shoe shop in town. Or maybe the assistant was just jealous of my spectacularly thin ankles and calves. I wanted Sindy's calves: sensible, substantial, fit-for-purpose, boot-wearing legs. That said, my relationship with Sindy didn't end well. I cut off her hair and her toes in a fit of pique one day. Maybe the sight of her oh-so-perfect boot-loving calves sent me over the edge. I do remember feeling ashamed of my actions. But I'd felt shame before, in Dolcis. And that's where all our beliefs about ourselves can start, with an odd comment innocently thrown out there to fill a gap.

We all live with shame. Shame about our bodies, shame that we can't control our cravings, shame that we take up too much room in the world. This is carried through to all addictions, be it drugs, sex, alcohol or any other. Shame, shame, shame, shame and guilt. There are situations where shame or guilt can teach us important lessons in life. They can make us effect change, remind us of boundaries we need to follow to function in society. But if they become a persistent, habitual stain on our own personality, they can lead us to believe we are repugnant, ugly, bad, unacceptable and, ultimately, unlovable.

How can we let go of those feelings of shame? For starters, it's important to remind ourselves that guilt is different from shame. Guilt is what we experience if we intentionally or unintentionally do something that feels wrong. But we can learn through guilt.

Guilt is feeling bad about what you did. Shame is feeling terrible about who you are. Shame is the result of a perceived belief about how other people see you, or what you have been told and how you have internalised that. It's not our own actions but our core being that is bad or wrong. Once we've internalised shame, every negative comment, every TV ad drip-feeds into the very heart of our shame tank. We tell ourselves, *I am ashamed of myself, so the rest of the world must be too. Therefore I will retreat and hide.*

How do we rid ourselves of these toxic feelings of being unworthy? We have to recognise that we are the keepers of the prison keys. We are the ones who are locking ourselves up in this cell of unworthiness. When we live with chronic shame, it often manifests and impacts on our entire body. Low self-esteem, depression, anxiety, eating disorders, substance abuse or co-dependency can steal precious moments of our lives. So how do we start to help ourselves?

One of the things that has helped me is becoming an observer in my own story, becoming a witness to my own thoughts. Notice when those toxic thoughts rear their heads, become aware: *Oh, here it comes. I'm a bad person. Is that really true?* Be compassionate. Catch yourself in the act of putting yourself down. I was never able to accept a compliment. Sometimes I still struggle. But back then, if the compliment took me away from my own rotten, rancid, cruel thoughts about myself, I would discount it. It's important to notice when someone says something positive, and even if you find it hard, say thank you and accept it graciously. It may feel completely fake and you still may not believe it, but by doing so you will learn to get more comfortable with it and will slowly become better and better at accepting and believing.

## TIPS

- Using food or drink (or cigarettes or drugs) to self-medicate is always only a superficial quick fix to feeling better – in the long run it might make things worse.
- When it comes to any form of addictive behaviour, make curiosity a habit. Question your old beliefs and ask yourself whether they serve you.
- Don't strive for perfection: small changes can bring about big results.
- Shame is a result of how we believe other people see us, or what we have been told and how we have internalised that. Remember that other people's opinions are just that. You can ignore them if you choose to.

# 14

## Imposter Syndrome

I don't belong.

I'm not good enough.

I don't deserve to be here.

How many of us have found ourselves suffering from imposter syndrome because of behaviours we've relied on all our lives? It might not be something we admit to openly, but I reckon most of us have been there, and it's a horrible feeling to have. And I definitely think it gets harder as we reach midlife and we start to wonder how we can compete in a world full of younger people with more time and energy. But what can we do about it?

The best thing to do with imposter syndrome is to take it and turn it on its head. After all, we are all imposters in that we don't know everything, we have more to learn, we have growing to do and things are unpredictable. Sure, we might get up every single morning and go to the same job, drive the same car, spend each day with the same colleagues or family, but every day is different – and so every day we are imposters in life from the minute we wake up. I don't see that as a bad thing, but that every day is full of opportunities. Being an imposter is exciting – who knows what's going to happen? What am I going to see today that

I've not seen before? What am I going to learn that I didn't already know?

As a young child I believed that I wasn't the right fit because there was something wrong with me. When I found myself at one of the country's top music schools was it because of my extraordinary violin and piano techniques? No, my father had got a job there as head of boarding. When the other kids laughed at my attempts to play, it only confirmed my belief that I wasn't good enough. My inner critic became a monster that hid away from prying eyes and tormented me when no one else was watching. The imposter syndrome was off the scale – it stayed with me well into adulthood.

How I wish I had known I wasn't alone in feeling this way. That I wasn't the only one out there thinking I wasn't worthy, the only one who had a strident inner critic telling me I wasn't good enough over and over. But as anyone who has been there will know only too well, shame (ah yes, that again) inevitably plays a huge part in all this, making it difficult to be open about it with family or friends – and so the monster continues to ooze its poison to contaminate moments of joy, and the vicious circle continues.

So what can we do to quieten it?

Mostly it boils down to awareness. When you notice it, you can start to do something about it. I think being a lot kinder to ourselves is half the battle too, as is seeing the truth – not our own personal fucked-up version. We should be mindful of our state of mind when we start searching for answers as to whether we are good enough. Imposter syndrome is just comparing ourselves to others, and if we didn't pit ourselves against others, the term wouldn't even exist.

Remember that our brains are incredible. We can rewire them, though compassion can be difficult to come by and we can find ourselves dismissing the positive too easily. But it's a bit like playing the piano: the more you practise, the better you become at it. It becomes a positive habit. Challenge your thoughts. Ask yourself, are they really true? What are you good at? What makes you unique? Keep practising and fake it till you make it.

Sometimes I think we are all a bit like babushka dolls, only revealing the face we want people to see and hiding our shame and insecurities deep within. Again, it's a case of remembering that we give life to our thoughts, but that's all they are, just thoughts, as we learned in Chapter 11 and beyond. We choose to give them the power, and the more we become aware of how we are helping to feed the monster, the less hold it will have. So when that negative voice starts telling you you're not good enough, you're not a nice person, catch yourself. Notice it. Tell yourself, *Oh, here we go again*, and learn to laugh at it.

You can also try mirror work: literally standing in front of a mirror and telling the monster to stop. Telling yourself that you don't need to accept these things because they are not true. You don't have to listen to that voice. You are doing okay. You have every right to be where you are, achieve the things you are achieving. It's also good to remember that, as midlife women, we have seen so much that we have wisdom based on lived experience, which can make it easier to break patterns that started when we were younger and didn't know or understand ourselves as well.

Another thing worth trying is giving the monster a name and drawing a picture of it. Give it life, see it as something other than you. That's what I did with the wine. It was something else that came up through doing Annie Grace's alcohol experiment: give life to that part of you that craves, that wants, that taps you on the shoulder. The part that creeps up and says, 'Wouldn't a glass of wine make tonight just perfect?' I found this really useful. I created my 'wine witch'; I drew her. When she told me that everyone at the party was having a good time because they were drinking, I could then picture this little person and tell her to back off. It's exactly the same thing when my inner critic starts telling me, 'You're not very good at this. Anyone could have done that,' and so on. I have a picture to remind myself that this is something separate from me and I don't need to give it any airtime.

We can be so critical of ourselves, say such terrible and mean things, but what we really need to do is be kinder to ourselves, our own biggest supporters.

What if I were to walk up to your best friend and say, 'You are an ugly, useless, stupid bitch.' How would you react? I would expect you would be horrified, shocked and appalled. No doubt you would jump to your friend's defence immediately – am I right? So why do we feel it's okay to say those things to ourselves? Why is it that so often the loudest voice in our head is a nagging, horrible, mean-spirited critic that condemns and stifles us? Where does it come from? Why do we listen to it? And more importantly, how do we quieten it?

If it has become a habit to constantly be down on ourselves, we need to unlearn those behaviours and see ourselves for who we *really* are. We are not broken, and every single one of us is loveable, is worthy, is valid. And that's what it's important to understand.

What does it mean to love ourselves? Pure love is who we are at our core. Pure love transcends superficial aspects and conditional love, be it familial, romantic or platonic. Pure love is unwavering and non-judgemental – but how often do we experience the feeling of loving ourselves unconditionally? We make life seem so complicated. I like to think that most of us are a great support to others; when we see someone who is sad, anxious, angry or overwhelmed, we empathise, we show compassion, we ask what they need at that moment. Do we do the same for ourselves? How many times have we said I'm useless, I'm pathetic, I hate myself, I don't deserve to be happy, I'm not a good person? We habitually tell ourselves we are not worthy – well, hello there, inner critic. We criticise ourselves for being radiantly flawed. Hallelujah, we are flawed. Pure love is non-judgemental and yet, in trying to access it, we are constantly judging ourselves. How ridiculous is that? To access that feeling we need to be kind to ourselves. We need to realise that that pure love is available twenty-four hours a day. It flows like water through us. We just interrupt that flow by damming it up with cognitive boulders.

This shift into introspection has made me realise how cruel I've been to myself in the past. I've constantly compared myself to others and always found myself lacking. I've made massive assumptions about everyone else while cherry-picking all the negative things about myself. It's been a constant battle and although I am now able to catch myself doing it more frequently, it still sneaks up on me because that's what being a human is all about. When that happens, I decide that everything I've achieved is a fluke. I'm a failure. I'm the worst parent, the worst wife, the worst daughter. I am unintelligent, untalented and people just haven't found out the truth.

Is that the case?

I hope there is plenty of tangible evidence to prove that none of that is true, but then part of me being a work in progress is that I still find myself in the position of having to respond to that critical voice when I hear it. I have to remind myself to say, 'Stop it, this is nonsense,' and then move on. And it feels really good to be able to do that.

Before this, as you've seen in the first half of this book, I thought that the best way to get people to listen to me was to make my presence overly forceful, but I needed to find a different approach.

My ex-husband, James – we've always been and still are brilliant friends – once said to me, 'Just because you shout doesn't mean you're right. Just because you shout the loudest doesn't mean you're going to win the argument. And you don't always have to win the argument.' It took me a very long time to accept that, though. I think I was just a very confused human and there was always that struggle to be heard. The fact I didn't know how to go about it made it all so much worse.

A huge part of my journey so far has involved taking a step back, starting to understand all this and learning to find my true voice. I've come a long way since the days I felt so lost, but even now with my mum, bless her, and my brother, I can still struggle with that need for validation. My parents were always very much don't-boast-about-anything kinds of people. They believed you should do things quietly and keep them private. So when I would ring up and say, 'I've just got this or done that…' they would just say, 'Oh yes, lovely,' and move on. I wanted them to say, 'That's amazing, well done!' I wanted to say, 'Please, please, please make me feel like I matter. That I've got something to say that's worth hearing. That I should be here.'

It was only when I stopped, took that step back and began to nurture myself, looking after little me, that things began to change. Now, when those old feelings creep back, I have learned to catch myself in the act and realise that this is about my perception of a situation, my 'reality' rather than the truth. If my monster tells me I am not worthy, if I feel that I need validation or that I don't matter, I know what to do. I remind myself that I have innocently created these thoughts. I do my best to catch them before they take over. I become more aware and recognise the thoughts for what they are. I self-soothe rather than looking externally to be soothed.

While outwardly I've always appeared to be quite a strong and determined character, inside I'm not sure I was ready to embrace that perception more widely until very recently. Part of it was definitely about being in the public eye. All the press intrusion and phone hacking scared the life out of me. So many people I work with have been through it and several still have ongoing cases. I really lived my life under the radar and a lot of that was down to fear, always thinking, *What if someone wrote something bad about me?* I've always been worried about what people thought of me and while it's a hell of a lot better now, there is still plenty of room for improvement. But I'm getting there. I've done the 'protecting my young' bit now, and that was definitely a very big part of it. Elliott is twenty-eight and over the whole 'cringing when people recognise me' thing. But as a kid he just wanted his mum to be normal and I completely get that. So I kept doing everything I could to make sure that my job didn't impact on his life. I also knew a lot of people in the industry who had been less worried than I was about putting stuff out there, and sometimes their kids got caught in the crossfire. I just thought, *I don't want my son reading things about me in the paper*.

That said, there was one time, a decade or so ago, when the nightmare did become a reality, but for that I have only myself to blame. I stupidly got in my car to drive home when I'd had a few glasses of wine. Before that I had never driven after even a single glass, but on that occasion I made a huge error of judgement. It was the culmination of what had been a very difficult period for me, but of course this was no excuse for my actions. Thankfully the police stopped me less than a mile after I'd set off. I spent a humiliating few hours at the police station, then went home and spoke to a couple of solicitors, but I decided very quickly that sometimes you have to hold up your hands and admit that you totally fucked up, which I had. Several weeks later I appeared in court to face the music, but the guilt stays with me to this day. On top of everything else, I had spent years keeping my head down and now I had embarrassed myself and, more importantly, I had embarrassed my family and my son. I vowed never to do that again.

These days I feel stronger and much more in control of things, and that has meant less of a need to hide myself away. I have also finally begun to trust myself to use my voice. I'd spent my entire life trying to find that trust in myself and it's only now I'm starting to find it. Other people might disagree, but actually, I think I'm all right. And at long last, I am able to start accepting the person I really am.

## TIPS

- Nurture yourself – it's only when you begin to look after *you* that things can begin to change.
- By the time you reach your forties, fifties and beyond, you have a huge amount of life and lived experience. This is an invaluable addition to the innate wisdom we all have within us.
- You should always own your mistakes.
- It's worth remembering that shouting the loudest usually gets you nowhere.
- You are good enough – you just need to believe it. Beware of searching outside of yourself too much, as that can lead you to believe that you are lacking. You are not lacking. Stop trying so hard – therein can lie the problem. Just be.

# 15

## I Don't Matter

Middle-aged friend wants to buy a car. Her car. Her money. She takes her husband along to the garage because they are going on somewhere afterwards and it's easier to go straight from there. She walks in and outlines exactly what she is looking for and what her budget is. The salesman ignores her and addresses all his questions and statements to her husband, while she is waving her chequebook frantically at the guy *right in front of her*, muttering, 'Yoo-hoo, I'm the one buying the car.' I have to say I thought those days were over, so I found this both surprising and hugely irritating. But then sometimes it does feel as though we barely register, doesn't it? We're a bit like flies, if you will, there in the background and to be swatted away when they get too close. I've even heard rumours that middle-aged women make great spies because nobody notices them.

This feeling of being invisible makes us midlife women feel isolated, angry, inadequate and out of touch. It can be unbelievably frustrating. We are ignored, we're written off and we're made to feel we don't count, even when we are – nominally – the ones who should be in control of a situation.

But where does this invisibility come from? Do others really have so little respect for women once they hit a certain age, when the odd grey hair or wrinkle first appears? I do think perhaps people have – wrongly – been subconsciously but habitually taught to think in this way and I find that exasperating, to say the least. But I also believe that at least some of it comes down to the fact that we women diminish ourselves when we age, because that's what *we* have been taught to do. We are conditioned to think that's how things are, that from now on it's normal that no one sees us, and so the whole stereotype is perpetuated. In this way, invisibility can come from inside out, not outside in, and we end up keeping ourselves prisoners based on expectation versus reality.

For some women, getting older can mean no longer giving a damn about what others think of you, and that can feel incredibly liberating. But when we're worn down by life, by lack of hormones, by work, by everything else we have on our plates, it can be what we think of *ourselves* that causes us many of the problems and can leave us feeling worthless. If that's the case, we have to address what's going on inside us as well as around us, and to look how we can stem the flow of negativity and self-sabotage.

We can become less visible with age because our priorities change. The way we look changes too, so we might tell ourselves we aren't as attractive any more. When we don't feel good about ourselves, it's a natural instinct to hide away because we don't really want to be seen. Or perhaps we've not been able to give ourselves fully to our careers because of kids – so we tell ourselves that we are not good at our jobs any more. It is in these small ways we start to define ourselves as invisible, less valued, less potent.

But there is no doubt that society has a lot to answer for as well. So often we women of a certain age are made to feel surplus to requirements, that we are almost disappearing from other people's vision, and perhaps nowhere more than in the workplace. This happens in pretty much every area of business you can think of. Maybe younger hires are cheaper. Maybe experience is not valued the way it should be. Certainly I see it in my own industry all the time; we get to a particular age and suddenly the roles diminish. There is apparently no audience for a 55-year-old (or a sixty-year-old or a seventy-year-old) lead actress. Instead, cameo parts are filled by well-known faces, now considered past their prime for the lead roles, and so the chances of a lesser-known actress – because we can probably count on one hand the Judi Denches and Helen Mirrens and women who transcend this – being cast diminish until yet another career is ended by society's ageism. In this way we see two groups of women diminished: the fading stars moving into ever smaller roles and the rest put out to pasture. We are expected to sit back and accept that our services are no longer required. To bow out gracefully while our male counterparts continue their careers but with our daughters now playing their wives. Or to be grateful for roles as difficult mothers-in-law, witches or dementia sufferers.

In this I feel privileged, because *Coronation Street* has a history of celebrating strong, matriarchal women – from Annie Walker to Elsie Tanner, and from Eileen Grimshaw to Gail Platt and beyond – and placed them at the forefront, and it's often the men who play supporting roles. But I know that I am in the minority. Outside soaps, decent roles for post-menopausal women are ever harder to find, which is bloody depressing and only seems to perpetuate the obsession with youth and underline the fact that we are out of date, past our prime. Yet again we are left feeling we don't matter.

I think it's very common for women to have a crisis of identity at multiple points in their lives. Whether it's because we've stepped back from a career to have a family, or we find ourselves pulled in different directions as part of the 'sandwich' generation; whether it's because we've hit middle age or are going through the menopause – all these life events can make us question who we are even more. But when you've always prioritised everyone else over yourself, perhaps even been a martyr to the cause of others (friends, children, partners) – and we've all done it – how do you bring value back to yourself?

It can take a long time to realise that we have put everything and everyone in our lives ahead of ourselves. But reaching that realisation is a good time to look at how things have evolved and changed over the course of our lifetime, and how we've got to the point we are at now. What does it say about us and our life as it is today?

I do think, certainly for those of us who are now middle-aged or older, that our culture has taught women and girls from an early age not to prioritise ourselves. And that there is a huge guilt associated with putting our needs above those of others. I know this is the case for me, though I don't think I was even remotely aware of it until I did take that step back and looked at it properly. I absolutely love my job, but a major part of taking the role in the first place came down to thinking that it would be perfect for us as a family – no more travelling away from home, no more constant auditions and thinking about what next – and that came before thinking about whether it would be perfect for me. Luckily it was, and it always has been – and I am immensely grateful for that – but that initial decision was far less about my needs and more about being able to be home for Elliott. To give him a secure routine. It's only now that I realise that that is an example of how ingrained it is in us as women to consider what's best for our families as much as what's best for us personally. I've been so fortunate in the way that it all worked out, but I appreciate this is not the case for everybody.

I think it's only now that I realise just how many times in my life there have been when I've put myself at the back of the queue, trying to make things easier for other people rather than considering the impact on my own mental or physical health this might have. I'm sure most of us have soldiered on when we are feeling under the weather, but I do think back to the time I went to work feeling absolutely rotten because I didn't want to let anyone down or cause them to reschedule any scenes. I was absolutely freezing, just couldn't get warm, even though it was the hottest day of the year. It was only later on that one of the other cast members happened to glance down and spot that my toes had turned blue-black. Turned out I had sepsis.

There's certainly a moral to this story. As women – and particularly as middle-aged and older women – we need to learn to look after number one. I have definitely got better at it, though, and I think I do have an underlying awareness that if I don't look after myself, then I will be of absolutely no use to those around me. That has been a really useful trait to have. You've got to learn to say 'no' more often. I have friends who have always, always put their family first or done what's expected of them even when it's been detrimental to their wellbeing. And it's when their kids have left that they go, 'Hang on, I'm not doing that any more. I'm not just going to say yes all the time.' Because so often we are conditioned to say yes. Yes, I'll do that, go there, sort that. Which is fine if you do want to do whatever it is, but not if you're just doing it automatically. Learning to say no, or I don't want to, is important. And I'm getting there. It's back to the old work in progress.

There is no doubt that our hormones (or dearth of) can throw a few curveballs into our path as we negotiate everything else that comes with midlife, and that can certainly add new uncertainty to the way we feel about ourselves. One symptom of menopause that many women experience is a loss of confidence, and that inevitably makes learning to value ourselves more difficult than ever. It probably doesn't help that menopause still seems to be seen as some grubby, secret 'illness'. I find it interesting that there are rituals and celebrations marking significant 'coming of age' events in our lives, be it birthdays, babies or the rest, and yet this is something we treat in a very different way. The fact that we grew up with conversations surrounding menopause being suppressed (let's face it – even our own mothers didn't share what they were going through, despite the fact one day we would have to go through it too) all helped to confirm that we are simply supposed to slink away quietly into the next phase of elasticated waistbands and incontinence pads. But I don't intend to slink anywhere, thank you very much.

By keeping these conversations behind closed doors, by not talking openly about menopause and ageing, we miss out on hearing so much about other women's experiences. Through this, and because of the way it's still somehow seen as slightly shameful, there is a danger that we end up painting a grim picture of it all and pushing ourselves further beneath our cloaks of invisibility. We can also perpetuate these attitudes unconsciously. I've often found myself laughing off the fact I have forgotten names or places by blaming menopause, when in fact I have always had a terrible memory for things like that.

I realise, of course, that for many women, the menopause can be a really tough time that has far-reaching impacts on all areas of their lives. But for others it can be relatively straightforward, and it would be good to hear those stories too. The long and the short of it is that all women will have different experiences and there is help available for those who need it (and yes, we need to know this). Thank heavens high-profile women such as TV presenter Davina McCall and doctors Nighat Arif and Annice Mukherjee are starting to change this, because these are discussions we need to be having, not only for our own sakes but for those around us as well. We need to know about this stuff, about women's real and lived experiences, not least so we are not reliant on what we read in the papers and online – information which can often be sensationalised or even plain wrong.

Women going through menopause are often busy working, trying to hold down jobs while sustaining relationships, caring for elderly relatives and taking on the lion's share of supporting kids and running a home – essentially being everything to everyone. We are meant to be desirable, practical, caring, empathetic; we are teachers, disciplinarians, nurses, partners, lovers, daughters, friends, sisters, economists, administrators, cooks, bottle-washers… the list is endless. Is it any wonder that sometimes – often – it all gets a bit much, and that's when things are going well. HRT might do the trick for many common menopause symptoms, but as Mukherjee says, 'it is not going to cure everything if you are smoking heavily or drinking heavily, or not sleeping properly, or on your phone late at night and stressed with work emails, or worrying about the health and wellbeing of your family.'

Midlife crises are nothing new, of course. But the world we live in now is very different from the one our mothers inhabited. They didn't have much of the labour-saving technology we rely on today and as a result they did more functional exercise and movement – both of which can be helpful in terms of dealing with the rigours of hormones. Their world was also less connected, which had its downsides, of course, but could also mean less stress because they didn't know what we were getting up to at university or when we were out and about with our friends. If we went travelling, sending the odd postcard was the norm and radio silence in between was not something our parents panicked about. But now we know every single thing our kids are doing, thanks to social media and the like, and while that has its plusses, that constant connection can be stressful, as we often know too much.

In terms of menopause, there are pros and cons to the media explosion. Programmes like Davina's McCall's *Sex, Myths & Menopause* and BBC Radio 4's *Woman's Hour* have been brilliant because that increase in awareness was long overdue. There have already been big steps forward as a result: the attention has prompted huge amounts of interest from major medical and other organisations, and seen people wanting to educate their staff and managers. Academic institutions like the Medical Research Council and the National Institute for Health and Care Excellence (NICE) have shown much-needed support in terms of menopause research. But there is collateral damage, and some of the good is being neutralised by the sharks on social media or brands that are making money out of women. One of the issues is that there is often a lot of fear around menopause or perimenopause, and women are made to feel that this is the end, because they are hammered with doom and gloom on social media and elsewhere. Mukherjee genuinely believes that a lot of that is also down to femtech, the commercial industry focused on women's health, which wants women to feel fearful, because if you're feeling fearful and see all these wonderful, glossy solutions online – aka clickbait – then you're going to keep clicking, and at the end of it you're going to have spent money. Far better to keep talking openly, and to speak to your GP if you are struggling.

Perhaps it's time for us to look at things differently, to think about our life experience and to see the maturity and self-awareness we have gained as a result as our secret weapons, our superpowers, if you will. It is these things that are key to allowing us to do and be whatever we want. We also need to remember that prioritising ourselves means valuing ourselves, and valuing ourselves means believing that we are deserving of love and respect. It means we are prepared to spend time investing in ourselves. If we do this, it, in turn, also impacts the relationships we have with others.

This is especially true when we are tired and overwhelmed by prioritising everything outside of ourselves, which is really useful to remember when we find ourselves in a low place, where our thoughts can become untrustworthy. For example, my husband used to say to me, 'We need to stop buying food and wasting it. That's the second bag of salad I've chucked this week.' If I'm stressed or overwhelmed, all I will hear is that he is accusing me of wasting food, or buying too much, or wasting money on buying more than we need. He hasn't actually accused me personally of anything, but that is what I have heard. When we are not looking after ourselves, we tend to make every little thing about ourselves. *He's criticising me. He's having a go…*

In fact, all that has really happened is my own insecurities and skewed thinking have been reflected back to me. When the thoughts get intrusive and loud in this way, we need to see it as a cue to notice what's happening rather than the content of our thinking, to realise that we are paying too much attention to our thoughts and not being in the moment, and to stop listening to our thoughts – because they sure as hell aren't reliable. Remember, thoughts come and go. If they are good, let them happen. If they are making you uncomfortable and anxious, notice and get present.

Here's the thing: it's all too easy to confuse prioritising ourselves with being selfish, to say, 'If I put myself first, then I'm selfish. If I say no to somebody, I'm selfish.' This leads us to the bigger question: do we value ourselves? Are we able to see what *we* need, what we are deserving of? This is something I've been asking myself a lot. Do I value myself, and in which areas? What do I need to do to value myself more?

I found it helpful to reflect on what valuing myself looked like for me. I definitely valued myself when it came to my voice being heard and standing up for myself, but in other areas I was lacking. I certainly didn't value myself or my poor body's health when I poured that red wine down my throat. We often think we are prioritising ourselves by having a long, hot bath, or by going to the gym, or by healthy eating or practising good sleep hygiene. Don't get me wrong – all these things are great, but they are external ways of putting ourselves first. What do they really mean at a fundamental level?

In order to truly prioritise yourself, you need to understand why you aren't ever putting yourself and your own welfare first: why might this be and what's stopping you from doing it? We need to be able to put ourselves in the present moment, to ask, 'What does it look like for me right now?' rather than paying attention to whatever is currently being bandied about on TikTok, whether it's ice baths or meditation. We just have to show ourselves love and compassion and non-judgement. The answers lie within every single one of us.

If you believe that we have a finite amount of love and compassion, then it follows that there is only so much to go around, that we therefore have to prioritise so many other people – children, parents, partners, colleagues, bosses – that it leaves nothing for ourselves. We get compassion fatigue. We become burned out… But the reality is that our supplies of love and compassion are endless and we never need to run out. It's our thinking around it that exhausts us. *Could I have done more? Should I have done more? Did I support so and so in the right way? Should I have done more to help today?* Shoulds and coulds ought to be banned! (I've even heard that there is a culture where the word 'should' and even the concept of it does not even exist. Lead me to it – now!)

Remember that bit in the safety briefings on a plane? There's a reason why they tell you to put your own oxygen mask on before helping anybody else. On this basis, why would you not prioritise yourself? By prioritising yourself, you are, by default, helping other people, because you have put yourself in a better place to do so. If you don't feel able to, ask yourself what this says about you – and what would happen if you put yourself first.

It almost goes without saying that it's often easier to bury our heads in the sand and not confront the things in our lives that need changing or challenging. But I've learned through my own experience that doing this can be the difference between surviving and thriving.

I certainly don't have all the answers, and I'm still very much on this journey myself, but I know what's worked for me so far, and I really do feel I've finally got a spring back in my step and a sparkle in my eye.

But what do we do about us as a whole, as a community of midlife women? Certainly we need to speak up, to change things. But it's not so easy to have an effect on society if we are still fighting internal battles about our own self-worth – and that's something we have to bear some responsibility for. We have innocently told ourselves that it's not our fault, but equally we have been made to fear stepping out of our boxes, those little areas we have been told we can occupy and be grateful for. And there you go, it's a self-fulfilling prophecy.

While we can lay the blame at other people's doors, we can't change the way that they behave. What we *can* change is how we deal with it – as the Austrian psychiatrist and Holocaust survivor Viktor E. Frankl said in *Man's Search for Meaning* (1946), 'When we are no longer able to change a situation ... we are challenged to change ourselves.' Think of our minds as though they are sat navs; you put in the wrong information and you're going to end up in the wrong place. In the same way, if we fill our heads with negative thoughts, then it's not going to make it possible for us to move forward to a positive outcome. We have to choose not to listen to the voice that tells us to stay under the radar, that told us to be grateful for every scrap and to know our limitations.

Change is happening. Slowly. It's good to see that there is now support offered by businesses for menopausal women, for example, but let's face it, it is often negligible. The damage has been done for so many years that for the average middle-aged woman it might all be a bit too late. So she won't be seen – but her daughters might be. Actually, she probably spends far more time making sure that her daughters know that they should be seen and that they should never allow themselves to be invisible. And yet she doesn't do that for herself. It's shocking that we have been made to feel this way.

Just keep remembering that we don't have to buy in to society's bias. When I realised – eventually – that every thought and belief comes from the inside out, I was able to change the way I responded to everything. And it's through that that I have been able to stop seeing my middle years – and beyond – as something to dread, but instead as a period of my life which offers promise, fulfilment and more.

As young women, we so often find ourselves rushing through our days at a million miles an hour. Nobody tells us that taking time to crowd out the urgency of life and to get to know ourselves better can help us find a peace that otherwise only happens with the passing of the decades and the maturing that comes (eventually, in my case) with age. But whatever our age, we cannot allow ourselves to get lost in the process. We matter, and we should never let anyone tell us any different.

## TIPS

- Put yourself first; prioritising yourself is *not* about being selfish.
- Life experience is a superpower – don't forget it!
- If you are struggling with the symptoms of menopause, ask yourself whether you are doing everything you can to support your menopause journey. And speak to your GP rather than falling down a rabbit hole of magic 'solutions' offered on the internet, or turning to private money-making clinics who make unrealistic promises.

# 16

## Stronger Together

I do feel sorry for women who are men's women – you know, the women who gravitate to the company and friendship of men over women. (And it's the *over* that's the point here – I have lots of male friends.) As I get older, I value both types of relationship but am more and more convinced that our priority should be to ensure other women are our allies and not our rivals.

Easy to say, I know. But as we move through to late middle age and beyond, we women have to have each other's backs. We need to celebrate our female friendships – the women who've lifted us along the way – as well as those rewarding moments of our lives when we've felt the joy of lifting others, particularly our contemporaries.

In as much as it's possible to do so, I've lived a relatively quiet public life. I've rarely given interviews; I've only just started an Instagram account. I've stayed beneath the radar wherever possible for reasons I explained earlier, and I've been lucky to – mostly – keep my privacy. Even so, being in the public eye has made me a target and a lot of the comments I receive are connected to the way I look. Would that happen if I was a middle-aged man?

Let's not even go there.

Of course, it would be easy to hold men wholly responsible for shaping the way we are viewed by society, but women can be – and are – part of the problem too and we need to stop giving each other a hard time and learn to support and uplift one another instead.

Recently, when I lost a fair amount of weight, I suddenly found I was being inundated on social media with people saying, 'Oh my God, what diet are you following?' 'How have you lost all that weight?' As I've said before, I don't believe in dieting, so please don't get me started. Diets only work while you are actively following them – trust me, I know! (Plus I never factored in the fact that red wine is not weight-friendly – something I only discovered once I stopped drinking it.) But to all those wonderful, kind people who contacted me via Instagram to offer compliments or to those who were obsessed with my diet – the answer is, I wasn't following one.

You know something? I actually hate this obsession with what other women look like. You know how it is when you walk into a room and they are like, 'You look amazing, you've lost so much weight,' and it just leaves you thinking, 'Did I look like a fucking dog before?'

Not long ago, a make-up artist said to me, 'Oh my God, you're like a different person. What have you done? Have you had surgery?' Their actual words. Oh, and don't get me started on the tabloids – they've been ringing my agent to ask for a comment on my facelift! I mean, thanks for thinking I've had a facelift, but I haven't and again, how dare you ask these questions!

You think someone looks fabulous? There are plenty of ways to compliment a human being without bringing weight into it. Some people, of course, revel in being told they are looking thinner, but I worry that this is only perpetuating the obsession and making people believe that thin = the only thing that matters, that physical appearance is everything. It puts so much pressure on other women, and we should be ashamed of ourselves.

But then this fixation on looks has been around forever. I remember when I was eleven years old and my mother took me to the doctor with a sore throat. I must have been sporting a school-day, scraped-back-hair look, because after taking my temperature and feeling my glands and dispensing the probably unnecessary antibiotics that they seemed to give out like Smarties in those days, the doctor (male) asked if we had ever considered having my ears pinned back. I mean, what the hell? I was there for a sore throat! It had never occurred to me or my mother that there was any issue whatsoever with my ears. I'm laughing as I write this now, but the audacity! How rude?! And yet – three weeks later I'm sat there in an iodine-soaked bandage finding it hard to balance the weight of my head after the procedure. I was like one of those nodding dogs you used to get on a car dashboard. I'd wanted one for years – who knew that I was going to become one? Going back to the ears, can you imagine that happening today? Although sadly, I possibly could.

All this becomes an even bigger thing as we get older, when change is inevitable, though when it comes to ageing and our self-image, we also have to bear some responsibility for the stories we've told ourselves. I know some women who are *so* hung up on turning sixty, panicking about what it will mean for them. Their self-worth is centred entirely around the façade of how they look and how they think other people see them. I know women who are having surgery because the thought of ageing is so abhorrent to them, so horrific and scary. If you want to have surgery, have surgery. If you want to use fillers, use fillers. I have no issue with that. But do it for *you*, not because you think this is how you need to be for other people.

Of course, none of this is anything new. Women have always looked for ways to 'enhance' their bodies and there's been pressure since time began for us to look a certain way. I find it depressing and terrifying in equal measure when I look back at some of the things we have felt we needed to do to conform with society's 'rules' or what others deemed to be attractive. The actress Joan Crawford was said to have had her back teeth removed to emphasise the hollows in her cheeks. In the seventeenth century women would use mercury to lighten their skin (and there are still mercury-containing products available to do this today). In the sixteenth century women would pluck off their eyebrows and pluck out their hairline to be more like Queen Elizabeth I – which was very much the look of the day. In the nineteenth century some women found themselves with deformed ribs due to wearing over-tightened corsets to look thinner, and screwed up their internal organs in the process. Victorian women used to put drops of belladonna – deadly nightshade – in their eyes to dilate their pupils and not only make their eyes look bigger, but also to make them watery to add to their air of fragility. They also bathed in arsenic to clear their skin. Then we have Chinese foot binding, and Renaissance women being bled with leeches to look paler, as that was thought to be more attractive. In the 1930s Isabella Gilbert designed a dimple-making machine, a process that was painful and didn't actually work, but women still gave it a go to get the indentations that they so desired. Georgian women put acid in their tea to get whiter teeth. The eighteenth-century version of bariatric surgery or diet pills was apparently tapeworms. And so it continues.

Nowadays, in conforming to society's view that in order to remain relevant we have to be – or appear – young, are we simply becoming our own worst enemies? It's a difficult one. Of course I understand wanting to look well as we age. I'm on telly. People see me on screen and I get my appearance commented on daily. I'll also happily share that I have had skin treatments, dabbled with fillers, a spot of microdermabrasion. Oh, and I also had a machine to suck a bit of fat out of my chin. That was brilliant. But I chose to do this after I'd done the work on the inside, and I did it for me – I don't care two hoots about what anyone else thinks about my face or the shape of my body. If it offends you, I don't give a shit.

Sometimes I worry about how young women today will deal with ageing. They are constantly force-fed unrealistic ideals. They have been raised in an era of social media where filler and filters and who knows what else lead us to believe that everyone else looks 'perfect' all the time. Will they end up being pressured into having their beautiful young smiles stretched into gargoyled pouts? And if so, what will happen when they reach sixty? Will our species evolve so faces never wrinkle, our lips so puffed and swollen you could balance an ornament on them? If you think that sounds outlandish, I recently met someone who had put so much filler into her lips that she had effectively disabled herself and could barely speak.

We can be our own worst enemies in conforming to society's view that in order to be relevant we need to remain young. We really don't. What we do need to do is engage our kids in this conversation. Show them where their true value lies. That confidence and self-belief are far more important than the outer package.

When we value ourselves, we don't compare ourselves to others. I'm endlessly fascinated by people (okay, nosy). There's nothing I love more than being a passenger in a car as we drive in the dark and seeing those tiny snippets of other people's lives in lit windows as we pass. It's a peek into another world and it instantly sparks my curiosity. I want to be a fly on the wall. How do their lives compare to mine? How different are they? What do you think they're having for tea? What do they talk about? Are they having a row? Do they love each other more than we love each other? There is a fine line between voyeuristic fascination (fun) and a comparison that leads to a spiral of self-doubt that can only ever make us feel worse about ourselves. We then find ourselves looking at everyone else, thinking they've got that bit of their lives sorted and we haven't. Not necessarily in a material sense, but in an emotional sense. How many times have I looked at a couple's life and gone, 'Oh my God, they're just so perfect, everything just falls into place for them, they're living the dream.' And then you find out that this was going on and that was going on… and it's just that public front that we all put on and that we all believe and get seduced by over and over again – when we should know better. So what do you do when you find yourself going off on that flight of fantasy? Bring yourself back down to earth. Look at them and think, *Yeah, well, I bet they still have skid marks in their pants*. Sometimes it really is as basic as that.

The fact is with age you realise that nobody is better or more special than you – and we need to stop identifying ourselves by the labels that have been imposed on us. She's the creative one. She's the athletic one. She's the academic one. If you are ever found lacking, in terms of not living up to those labels, you are going to feel crap. We often judge ourselves by our identities (for example, the adopted one) and through this we can create bad feeling and pain for ourselves. What we need to focus on is what we are – not who we identify as. We are energy within a body with the most incredible ability to think and create the lives we want. We should value ourselves and others for this. And that is our superpower.

We are a sisterhood, but one of the worst traits we have goes back to our limbic lizard brain, which tells us it's all about the survival of the fittest, keeping our line going. The result is that we can be so cruel to each other and we can create divisions ourselves. But we also have the power to change; we can change our mind at will. We don't need to be defined for ever by the way we or others might see us at any given point of time. When I was seventeen I wanted to live in Canada and be a nanny. When I was nineteen I wanted to come home and go to drama school instead. That's what you do when you're young and are a bit confused. But now that you've reached fifty, sixty, seventy... be what comes to your mind and not what you think you should be. We innately know who we are, and if we are not happy, we can change it. If you want to be less judgemental, be less judgemental. If you want to be kinder, be kinder. Life is about finding the joy within you.

Fellow Loose Woman Christine Lampard and I were chatting the other day and admitted to each other that our guilty pleasure is watching shows like *The Real Housewives of Beverly Hills*. I'm completely fascinated by the fact that these women seem so hideously shallow, and even though it's not a drama like *Corrie*, they too are expected to play their parts: the kind one, the villain, and so on. I'm cringing all the way through, but I can't stop watching it. It makes me realise that people haven't changed since the playground. If you want to be noticed or get anywhere, you've got to be in the right gang. You've got to wear the right shoes. And it makes me think – *Really? Have we not evolved as a species to do better than that?*

It takes me back to the time when I was thirteen and my mum took me shopping for shoes (why do so many of my terrible teenage memories involve footwear?!). It was always a nightmare, as even at that age I had massive feet, which were the bane of my life. Try finding half-decent school shoes in a seven and a half back then. Horrendous. So off we went down Market Street, in and out of shop after shop, and of course no one had my size in any of the ones I liked. My poor mum, she'd be 'What about these?' and I'd be really bolshy and say no. 'These are nice?' she'd try again. I replied that I wouldn't be seen dead in them and my friends would laugh at me if I wore them. My mum rolled her eyes. 'This is ridiculous. It's a pair of shoes. Just try them.' One day I dug my heels in further and said I wouldn't even try them because they were crap. And that was the final straw for my mother, who turned round and slapped me in front of all the people in Debenhams, all the other teenagers trying on shoes. Oh my God, I wanted to die. And all over the fact that the shoes weren't what I thought other people would think I should be wearing.

My whole belief system revolved around the fact that I didn't belong. Now I can see how wrong that was. It was ridiculous. But at the time it consumed me, and it's taken me years to realise that and that there is a big difference between belonging and fitting in. When you constantly make yourself fit in, you are constantly betraying yourself for other people. Belonging never asks us to change who we are. It demands we be who we are. We need to find peace in that. We need to be kinder to ourselves and kinder to each other. Support rather than judge. Cheer rather than sneer. The sisterhood matters, and whatever our age, we all need to play our part. And that's never truer than when we reach middle age and beyond, so that we become a more visible force to be reckoned with.

## TIPS

- Focus on what you are, not what you think others might define you as.
- Avoid comparing yourself to others – too often it just leads to a spiral of self-doubt. Put the energy into valuing yourself instead.
- Find evidence of how your own personal thinking is creating your reality. Notice how your feelings fluctuate as they are led by the thoughts you pay attention to.
- Remember that focusing on the here and now is the only way to create the space to allow another thought to pop up.
- If you decide to make physical changes or enhancements, do it for *you* and not for anyone else.

# 17

## A New Way of Thinking

You know what's a really good thing to do? To become comfortable with being uncomfortable. It's okay to say, 'I can't feel positive right now' – being positive all the time is exhausting. But recognise that this is how humans work and know it will shift. I can't tell you how much this mind-shift has helped me. I have more peace of mind. The chatter has quietened and thoughts don't last anywhere near as long. I'm able to remind myself that it's my thinking behind the feeling and, most importantly, that I do not have to engage with the content of every thought that turns up. I also take my moods less seriously than I used to.

We all have a wonderful gift in that we are able to reinvent ourselves. Let me use myself as an example. When I looked at pictures of myself, what I saw on the outside pretty much represented what was going on inside. I never felt okay. I would constantly beat myself up and find fault with everything about myself. And yet I wore a perfect mask so no one else would ever have known this. Reinvention starts the same way as everything else – with one little thought: *I wonder what it would be like to feel…* Reinvention feels like a huge, mammoth task, too big a mountain to climb.

But you just start with getting curious and the magic will follow.

Breaking patterns only becomes a problem if we think of the thoughts as negative. We need to remember that our thoughts don't have form, that they are neutral. I thought I hated the gym. Turns out I don't at all. I just believed I did. I started my gym journey constantly saying, 'I don't want to go to the gym. I don't like it. I don't enjoy it.' But on the days my inner voice said those things, I ignored it and went anyway, and then came away feeling great. Behind every thought is a feeling and behind every feeling is a thought.

So now you might wake up in a sad mood or a bad mood and wonder why you are feeling unhappy or disgruntled and what's caused it. But within those wonderings are those little sparks of inner wisdom that will help you understand you don't need to interfere. They might direct you to get up, to have a shower, get dressed, and reset. It's a bit like a photocopier. You press print or start and wait for it to do its job. If you start pressing all the buttons, you know it's going to end up jamming.

It took a long time for me to get here – a meandering and lengthy route if ever there was one – but the Three Principles has helped me to understand that my thinking had been distorting my real life, that compelling thoughts happen when you're most upset, that impulsivity happens a lot when you are in a low mood. And that process of going back and waiting and listening to my own insights and wisdom has made so much difference. Oh, and when I say wisdom, I'm not talking about academic intelligence or degrees or doctorates here, but the innate wisdom we all have within us.

I spent way too long thinking that the intellectuals, the ones with certificates and letters after their names, were the ones who could give me the answers I sought, not understanding that true wisdom is available within all of us. My search went on for years as I looked outside myself all the time. I tried everything from meditation (the act of which was useful until the practice was over), to various weird and wonderful sessions and weekends away to try and quieten the voices. I tried yoga – and let me tell you overthinking and trying to do sun salutations at the same time was absolutely exhausting. None of these worked for me. They simply formed part of the act of searching. Learning that so many of our problems come from within and that I could change the way I thought about things to get through them was a revelation. I stopped constantly searching for solutions by only going back over the past; that was simply helping to keep difficult things alive and making it difficult for me to get rid of that pain. Just taking a step back and recalibrating can really make a difference.

We all have millions of thoughts every day. Can we remember them all? No. The ones that seem important are the ones we give life to, give energy to and value to. You can think anything you like – for example, have you ever had that feeling when you get to the edge of a cliff where you think, *Ooh, I wonder what it would be like to just jump* (a friend says that whenever she goes to the theatre and sits in the circle it's the same). Perhaps you think, *I want to murder my husband*. Or, *I'll jump in front of this car, then they'll be sorry*. We all have things like this that flit through our brains, but it's about whether you choose to act on these thoughts rather than just think them. When you do give your negative thoughts power, it can be all too easy to end up in a state when you really don't need to. That fight-or-flight sense of panic might have been useful back in the days when we were cave people and running from a tiger. But in our world today, the threats are very different, and we therefore need to find different responses to avoid ending up as a great big ball of stress.

Here's another example. I might think, *I've got so many lines I need to learn for tomorrow. How many have I got? Look, ten scenes. Oh my God, I had eight scenes yesterday and that nearly killed me. How am I going to learn all that? I can't believe they gave me so many scenes yesterday when they know how many hours I've been doing. There must be a reason they've given me all those lines. Maybe they want me to trip up. Maybe they want me to fail. Oh God, why? Maybe I can't act. Maybe they think I'm shit. Am I shit? Does everyone think I'm shit?* And just like that, I've gone from 'I've got a busy day' to 'my career is over' in less than a millisecond of thinking time.

This happened to me a lot when I was younger. I chose to hold on to the content of my thoughts and in hanging on to that, I would start to get anxious. In these circumstances our brain will think, *Shit, there is a problem*. It decides there is a threat, so it creates adrenaline, increases our body temperature and heart rate, and although adrenaline surges only last a very short time, about eight minutes, there is still plenty of opportunity for our thoughts to remind us that we are panicking, that our palms are sweating, our heart is racing, and so on. This tells our brain that the adrenaline is not enough, so it therefore produces more until we get to the point where our lizard brain thinks this is a very serious situation, the lion or the tiger is nearly upon us. It sends in the big guns and it makes cortisol.

Cortisol is a hormone produced by the adrenal gland which is brilliant at helping our bodies cope with stress. But if we pump out too much for too long, instead of being beneficial, it can become harmful instead. It can impact on the production of other hormones that we need, which in turn suppresses our immune system, which is why we get colds or infections when we are stressed and run down. It will play on our weaknesses – mine is always my throat or my chest. So we have to be aware of how we and our thinking impacts on our bodies. Our body takes what we think as gospel, so we have to do as much as we can to modify our environment and control our perceptions around everything. We are all guilty of ignoring the signs when we don't prioritise ourselves. We get overwhelmed, depressed, anxious, and through that we set off all those systems in our brain. If we don't take action to quieten down our thinking, our body will simply send us more and more symptoms, which will get louder and louder as long as we don't listen. When it comes down to it, it's all about survival. Our brain thinks it's protecting us. But we need to pick up on these cues and take responsibility for the role of our thinking in all of this. We need to learn when to retreat and reset.

It sounds so simple when you put it like that, doesn't it? In reality it can mean having to unlearn behaviours that we have carried with us for far too long. We all have stories and patterns that often, as an adult, don't serve us well, but which have become so habitual that they are ingrained in us, a part of us. So we say things like, 'It's just what I do,' or, 'This is how it's always been,' or, 'This is who I am.' But this is the perfect time to make a change, to say to yourself, 'It's always been like this: this is who I am *until now*.' 'All those habits, those things where it's just what I do – that is, *until now*.' 'I've always been an anxious person *until now*.'

We get attached to our beliefs because they are familiar and we come to believe them, to the point they are reaffirmed by others. It's a cycle of repetition, and I love that life gives us endless possibilities to change that.

The thing to remember is that thoughts are a bit like taxis – and you can choose which one you get into. Or think of them as eateries, and again it's your choice which you visit. You're on holiday and there's a whole line of restaurants with people outside trying to entice you to come in. 'Hey, over here! We specialise in paranoia. Everyone hates you in here.' Or, 'Over here! We do a great "Oh God, the menopause is shit, isn't it?" special.' Or, 'Come to this one. We've got a great two for one on "I'm getting anxious",' or, 'How about here for some physical symptoms?' You choose which restaurant you go into and you eat a bellyful of whatever they are offering. But you need to remember that if the food's not good, you can send it back or you can leave – and it's exactly the same with thinking. If you don't want a smorgasbord of toxic thinking, you can choose to walk past that restaurant and not to go into it at all.

It's all about using our inner wisdom to change the narrative. My friend Sarie, who introduced me to the Three Principles, said, 'What if every human on the planet, whether male or female, were to experience anxious thinking at 3 p.m., wherever they were in the world? What if we all had this anxious thought, we all felt it at the same time, in the same way, at the same intensity? Would we be as bothered by it? No. Because we'd all say, "This is just what happens at 3 p.m. It might be uncomfortable, but we know what it is and we accept it."' And so its potency is reduced.

Being a work in progress – or in Sarie's words, 'perfectly imperfect' – there are still times when the impulsivity takes over, but at least now I can recognise it for what it is. Here's an example: sleep is pretty important to me. I mostly sleep well, but my thoughts around it used to trip me up. I'm an early-to-bed person and, understandably, other family members are not. So there were times when Brian and Elliott had been out to a gig and I would hear them come in, bang about in the kitchen and then put music on. I would repeat the same scenario again and again: get out of bed, go downstairs, tell them to be quiet – and then everyone was left feeling bad. They felt resentful of me ruining their fun night. I felt resentful of my sleep being interrupted. These feelings would carry over to the next morning, meaning that everyone was still slightly grumpy.

Alternatively, I could have pre-empted any issues by thinking back to the times it had happened before and instead dealt with it in a calm and constructive way. I could have listened to the wise little voice that was saying let it be, use ear plugs or headphones to tune out, and then rolled over and gone back to sleep, content in the knowledge that they'd clearly had fun. But I didn't. I ignored that insight, that little bit of awareness that was telling me what to do. I knew if I listened to my wise voice, it would not only make things better but I would feel proud of myself for listening to it. I understood it was a pattern of behaviour I could change and that I would see the positive impact accordingly. Instead I was grouchy, which spilled into the next day – which was totally unnecessary. Lesson learned. Always listen for the wisdom and ignore that impulsive 'I must take action immediately' noise in your head.

There's a Syd Banks quote I love: 'If your thoughts wander to a rocky and negative path, don't take them too seriously. Refrain from analysing yourself, because you will analyse yourself forever without reaching an end, and bitterly fail to find peace...'*

Have you ever walked through one of those Halloween 'haunted houses'? You move from room to room knowing that at any minute something shocking is about to happen. You pull your coat or scarf over your ears – or at least I do – because to me (and don't ask why) having my ears covered always meant the monsters couldn't see me. No, me neither. Anyway, you're on high alert, your heart is thudding and you feel fear, real fear. You cling on to your friend for support and the tension builds until it's unbearable. Everything is being experienced as though it's happening in reality. You hear a chainsaw revving and it's *The Texas Chainsaw Massacre*. You see the man in the mask and you scream, you start to run, but there is a part of you that says, *Hang on. This is just a game. It's not real and it's not going to hurt you*. That is what wisdom sounds like. If you stop listening to the content of your thoughts and quiet your thinking down, you can hear that voice. And when you do that, and are able to see that it's just thought rather than reality that you're experiencing, it's like having a Get Out of Jail Free pass.

When we become overwhelmed and stuck within the content of our thoughts, we just need to bring out this card and remind ourselves that we are the creators of the stories in our heads. They might terrify us, but with our quiet wisdom we are able to soothe ourselves.

Wisdom is there in all of us but so often we don't see it. We need to listen to it, to know that noise can get in the

*From *The Missing Link: Reflections on Philosophy and Spirit*.

way, but you can learn to find the quiet and understand where that wisdom lies. We don't need to follow everything that comes into our heads, whether it's about drinking, eating, relationships or anything else. We don't need to act on every thought we have.

We all know people who are addicted to the drama of their life. Their thinking is so warped that they cannot and will not consider that maybe they have it wrong. They can't see that the choices they have made have led them to where they are today. They have become addicted to their own unreliable and untrue thought system, so the idea that their thoughts can be responsible for their place on this planet is unimaginable. Yet we are all guilty of it until we wake up and smell the coffee and realise in fact that it's not coffee after all, it's actually tea. And there are so many sayings out there to remind us we can't see the wood for the trees.

There's a great analogy about thinking of your life as a big picture painted on canvas. Our thoughts shape our experience like brushstrokes on that canvas. If we couldn't think, it would be like having a blank canvas. No colours, no strokes, no way to understand what's happening.

Judy Sedgeman, former psychologist and now a Three Principles practitioner, suggests we imagine a fire in the house across the street. How do we feel about it? What we think will determine whether or not we will freak out about it. Am I afraid it will spread to my house? Will I run over to see if I can help? Shall I dial the fire brigade or assume someone else has already done it? There are a million different ways we can respond to bad things, but our response is not generated by the event itself: it's caused by the thoughts we have about the event, which become real to us. As I've mentioned before, having negative thoughts is part of life, of being human. They can fill us with fear and anxiety and insecurity.

Life can be hard, but we choose how we experience it. Think of memory as AI that you programmed yourself. It looks like truth because you created it, but in reality it's just beliefs. Memory is invaluable – I couldn't do my job without it! But it's only useful if you use it when you need it. We need to live in the moment. Kids do it naturally. If we constantly find ourselves living in the past, then we are simply living dead thoughts. They are gone. They're no longer real. The world doesn't change: it's our view of the world that changes. That's the most important thing to remember.

So what helps us get into a better state of consciousness? Essentially, anything that takes you away from your head. And if you can step back and watch yourself, you gain perspective and clarity. If you like, you gain a bird's-eye view of your journey.

At this point I should stress that all this is not about *not* having negative experiences. Those are part of life and something we all have. It's about understanding how we as humans work. When we are in those low moods, if we can access our innate wisdom, we can be kinder to ourselves and the negative thoughts may not spiral out of proportion so often. When we realise that the negative thoughts are coming from within and start to observe them, we are able to bounce back quicker. As I've said, we don't get so wrapped up in the drama. We see it for what it is – just thoughts that will pass.

Lucy Hone, director of the New Zealand Institute of Wellbeing and Resilience, said in a TEDx talk that 'resilient people get that shit happens'. They know that the oh-so perfect lives we see on Instagram are not reality and shouldn't be used to shape our own expectations – and that suffering is part of every human's experience. They are able to realistically assess situations, focusing on the things they can change rather than on the things they can't.

This so easily applies to women of a certain age. This new way of looking at things, of regrouping and moving on, has been absolutely key to me finding my own way forward to a stronger, brighter and happier future. It made me realise that, actually, I have always been very resilient, and I have proved it over and over again in my life. I have always made my own decisions without relying on other people's opinions. I have always followed my dreams without caring whether they aligned with other people's expectations. I have made my own rules, I have reflected, I have tried to improve my personal wellbeing. I have always challenged myself, I have always advocated for myself. I've always been incredibly independent. My only problem? That I just couldn't see it. But it really was that fucking simple. What an insight that was.

I spent years being the life and soul of the party. To be at peace I had to constantly be distracted – planning, cooking, hosting. I was the instigator, the party-giver, the dinner host because, quite frankly, any escape from myself was better than nothing. If only I could have seen that I was creating this unhappy place with my own thoughts. I just believed they were true, and my brain tricked me over and over again. But I didn't *have* to listen to the thoughts: I could have seen them for what they were. I spent years and years trying not to be me, to get away from myself, but that was then and this is now. Now I have learned that I don't want to be that and I don't need to do that. It doesn't serve me, so let somebody else take up the gauntlet.

Now I long for Sundays, I long for a day of no commitments and quiet. I love time with myself, and everything I do now is because I want to do it, not because I'm trying to escape myself. And you know, I like my quieter, more reflective self. Call me boring, call me dull, I don't care. I'm giving myself everything I need and following the paths that make me happy, and I feel saner and calmer for it.

I have now learned to be me – and I like it.

## TIPS

- Remember that you can always use your inner wisdom to change the narrative.
- Believing something to be true is not always the same as it actually being true.
- It's important to remember that where we as humans get things wrong is by believing that our feelings are caused by everything coming at us or happening to us. The reality is that we are only ever experiencing our thoughts.
- When we realise the content of our thoughts isn't something we need to make sense of, it's easier to let those thoughts pass.
- You can choose to move away from negative thoughts.
- The lifespan of an actual thought is only as long as you think it, not a moment longer.

# 18

## Breaking Away From the Comfort Zone

As we get older, it's all too easy to cling to the familiar and to not want to step outside our comfort zone. When we are presented with opportunities or new things or change, we so often find ourselves turning them down, saying things like 'Oh I couldn't' or 'I'm not brave enough.' And this got me thinking. We look around the gym and there are so many people focusing on their physical health, measuring their body composition, building muscle. Or we become slaves to our Fitbits and obsessed with counting steps. But how much time and effort do we put into making sure we are also the best we can be mentally? How do we make these changes in our minds, not just in our bodies? How can we make sure we can follow our dreams, whatever they might be and no matter how large or small? How do we find the bravery we need to adapt to change or confront situations that are not making us happy?

We get stuck in ruts because change can be scary. The changes needed to get what we want can seem too big or inaccessible and we might feel that we don't have the courage or the ability. But we do. We all do. Courage isn't something that some people have and others don't. It's within us all. Courage, bravery, call it what you will, doesn't just appear overnight. It's exactly like going to the gym, a muscle that needs to be exercised, that requires strength conditioning. It can take time; when I started going to the gym I was knackered after ten minutes, now I'm knackered after thirty. But that's still progress.

Whatever we dream of doing or achieving, it's so easy to find a million excuses why we can't do it. I've left it too late. I don't have the money. It's the wrong time. The chance has gone. I'm scared… But it's perhaps the most important time to keep up the idea of constantly challenging ourselves – those challenges often offer reinvigoration or new excitement about life. The truth is, we're all scared. It's normal to be scared unless you're Superman (and even he has the odd wobble!). But if you start exercising that courage muscle, you'll be amazed at what it can do. Start small – today I'll commit to doing something outside my comfort zone. That could be as simple as a phone call to enquire about an evening class, it could be joining a book club, or starting something that you would normally not do. And the more you do those small tasks, the more normal they become. And the courage bicep just gets bigger and stronger.

I've spent too much of my life holding back through fear, but now I'm able to do things even though I'm scared – by reminding myself that being scared is a feeling I've created through my thoughts and I choose to ignore the thoughts and just do it. If I sat and pondered too much about all sorts of things, I wouldn't do any of them – so the simple answer is that I no longer allow myself to do that. The old me would not have entertained the idea of taking part in *I'm a Celebrity, Get Me Out of Here* for a second. The new me? I'm not saying it was the simplest of things to say 'yes', but one thing is for sure: I will never regret finding myself on that plane to Australia and heading for the depths of the jungle. So what brought about this change?

Here's the bit about me that I want to share, although it's hard for me to do so. But I know other women feel this way too – perhaps for different reasons, but they feel it.

I was scared, absolutely – but I wanted to push myself out of my comfort zone to embrace the unknown and discover more about myself. I knew I'd be out there as me and not Eileen, which was daunting, but I decided it was something I needed to do. It was a rare opportunity and it was a privilege to be asked. I felt like if I turned it down, I'd be saying, 'That's it now, I'm nearly sixty and nothing's going to change.' I'm thrilled I did it, though – it made me braver and taught me a lot about myself. Now I need to have more adventures. I'm not going back to saying 'no' to things; it's too easy for that to become the default, to stay in our safe little worlds, and I think that's the case for a lot of women of my age.

If you're not sure whether to go for something, try tossing a coin. When I was going back and forth with the 'should I or shouldn't I say yes to *I'm a Celebrity*?', that's exactly what I did. Was I was going to let the random way that coin landed make my decision for me? Absolutely not. But sometimes it's a brilliant way to understand what we really want the answer to be.

Heads I say yes, tails I say no.

It lands on heads and I am delighted, so I know that is the right decision. It lands on tails and I feel disappointed. Then I know that deep down it is something I really want to do. And so it proved to be – despite the fact that before I went into the jungle I believed that I was terrified of snakes and creepy-crawlies. In fact, I was so worried I even went for hypnotherapy in the run-up to the show – which did help me relax in many ways and did calm my brain when I was attending the sessions. All the same, I'd already decided exactly how I would feel when I came face to face with my dreaded foe: anything creeping, crawling or slithering. I was one of those people who couldn't even touch a snake on the page of a book. I'd have a visceral reaction. If anyone played a prank or threw something resembling a snake in my direction, I'd scream. I'd literally see and feel this thing landing on me, I'd feel the disgustingness of it, and I'd run around brushing off the image of this hideous creature on my back. Or I'd imagine maggots crawling into my ears, into my clothes, over my body. It was an all-consuming dread and fear, and yet I'd never actually experienced any of these things. They were all stories I'd created in my head, my perceived reactions. They weren't real. I terrified myself by creating a story about how vile a snake feels, how slimy a maggot or a worm was and how I would react, and demonised them all. And that's what humans do. We see something in our mind's eye and therefore believe it to be true.

But the reality was actually very different and not half as scary. I mean, plunging my hand into a box full of mealworms and maggots and cockroaches is never going to be my activity of choice, but it was certainly nowhere as bad as I'd ever imagined. My thoughts had created my fears, but then my experience changed those thoughts. I no longer have ill feelings towards creepy-crawlies or snakes. I changed my mind about them all. And that's the glorious thing about us humans. We can have different thoughts. It's hardwired into us – it just happens. Being aware of this is a huge comfort in times of pain or stress. None of us can control all of our circumstances, and all of us will, of course, experience sad, bad or awful times. But just knowing that a new thought or feeling will come along can really help us deal with those tough moments.

Once we got into camp life on *I'm a Celebrity*, we completely forgot that there were cameras filming our every move and just got on with things regardless. Everything became routine, and with twenty-four hours a day to fill with nothing to do except washing yourself or cooking beans – unless you were the person doing the trial to earn stars and win food for the camp – you get caught up in the boredom and the mundanity, and don't really think about anything else. So in that moment round the camp fire when I told my adoption story, I didn't consider that there would be people at home watching. I suppose that's why the series works so well, though, because you get to see aspects of people that you would never normally see because they have forgotten that they are on camera.

I think we all did really well when we were out there. We were a pretty cohesive group and, on the whole, quite grown up. It's an extraordinary thing to meet a whole bunch of strangers and then, over a three-week period, they become your family. Confidences are shared. You make friends with people you never imagine you would or could become friends with. I think what really worked for us was that we operated as a team – we naturally let people play to their strengths, while retaining a sense of fairness. I don't remember a proper argument amongst us.

News broadcaster and fellow Loose Woman Charlene White was motherly, amazing at keeping track of the rice and beans, meticulously ensuring we were never in a situation where we'd run out of food if we didn't get any stars. Charlene brought her siblings up, and in this situation her caring and efficient manner came to the fore.

Rugby star Mike Tindall was our 'man make fire' person, a constant who would wake in the middle of the night to ensure the fire lasted until morning. He was definitely my rock. We had an easy friendship that just grew naturally, and he made us feel safe.

Footballer Jill Scott and *Hollyoaks* actor Owen Warner, although adults, were, I guess, our 'kids' – both beautiful souls who lacked cooking experience. This was remedied by giving them cooking responsibilities, and they surprised themselves with their skills. They were joyous, young and fun. Jill is just a genuinely lovely, decent person with a big heart. What you see is what you get. There's no side to her. She was a brilliant campmate, and I really wanted her to win.

Owen was always starving, and my motherly instinct kicked in, so I was always giving him a bit of my rice and beans, as I found him being hungry distressing. In fact, he was so hungry and getting so thin that I decided to try and win him the beach barbecue via helicopter. In the end it came down to chance, and I bloody won it; I was devastated. The boy needed food. But it was me, politician Matt Hancock and Jill who flew out of the jungle to the beach, where there was a whole table groaning with food.

We were warned not to eat too much as we had got used to having so little food, but I have to say that Matt's barbecue skills were second to none. Matt Hancock on the grill – I'd buy it. We also managed to secrete a stash for our campmates. Jill had sirloin in her bra. Matt had produce in his pockets and under his hat. I had half a loaf in one pocket and emptied the salt cellar into another. Nobody said a word. We arrived back at camp. TV presenter Scarlette Douglas, another campmate, can use British Sign Language, and I could just about sign the alphabet, so I signed to her to say, 'Take the pot to the dunny [toilet] – we have food.' She dutifully sauntered off with the cooking pot as if to rinse it and placed it just inside the hessian sacking door of the dunny. We then popped in one by one to drop our stash into the pot and that night the camp ate really well. Although I do remember getting a bit cross with Matt as he asked for a share of the food; he'd eaten a bloody smorgasbord during the day, for God's sake.

Scarlette was always enthusiastic, keen, involved and fun. Baba (as comedian and actor Babatunde Aléshé was always known) I found hysterical. I'd glance across at a man brooding, sitting deep in thought, contemplating – and then suddenly there'd be this burst of energy and he'd have us all crying with laughter. Radio X presenter Chris Moyles – I love that man. He wasn't at all what I'd imagined, he was gentle, kind and funny. Someone you could call on for anything.

Comedian Seann Walsh and I formed a strong bond and quite often played out little sketches together. He's probably most like me when it comes to humour. Seann needs to be kinder to himself. He has such a huge heart. And as for singer Boy George… George is just George. As people saw on camera, he would regularly threaten to walk, then reappear fifteen minutes later as if nothing had happened and with a smile on his face. Some of the others would worry when he disappeared, but I always knew he was capable of regulating himself and doing what he needed to do in the moment. Taking himself off for that short period of reflection always did the trick. Chanting really helped him too. In fact, it was only after about a week of hearing this really strange bird call in the morning that I was informed it was actually George's breathing exercises and not some exotic Australian bird.

As for Matt Hancock, I think it was unfortunate for him that Covid was still very much at the forefront of the public's minds, and the anger and resentment were so raw. Some of the policies he had implemented had directly impacted members of our own jungle family in the most devastating ways. It was still a massive thing and we all had to spend ten days in isolation before we were even allowed to head into camp. We had heard the rumours – I think George brought it up first – but we thought that's all they were, rumours. So it was still a shock when Matt walked in.

We were put in a very difficult position. Should we bring up his actions as health secretary during the pandemic? If we didn't, we knew we would be slated by the public, so we couldn't ignore it just for the sake of an entente cordiale in camp. The conversations had to be had, but in a way, we were damned if we did and damned if we didn't, as we were stuck there together. Having a newsreader in the fold really did help, though. Charlene basically interviewed Matt, we dealt with it, and then we moved on, at least for the duration of the camp. There was no backstabbing, despite what the tabloids said. There were the usual irritable moments that happen when a group of people are thrust together in a unique experience with limited food, little sleep and twenty-four hours to fill. But I'm proud of how we coped. I suppose my role became a sort of camp counsellor, and I hope I was able to lend support when anyone had a wobble. And we all had one. It was impossible not to, whether it was Charlene feeling she'd let her kids down by not managing in a trial, or Seann doubting himself. But we all did the best we could.

Incidentally, we were trolled by a very small minority on social media saying that we bullied Matt. This was absolutely not the case – ask Matt, he was there! – and a perfect example of people's beliefs being based on watching an out-of-context twenty-minute edited version of a twenty-four-hour period. Essentially trolls deciding to dislike or hate based on nothing but their own thought-created reality.

Matt took on all the trials, which wasn't really great for the team. We all came in fired up and prepared to do different tasks, to face our fears, to prove ourselves. But the audience kept on voting for him. As time went by, we got more tired, weaker, hungrier and the fire inside us started to burn less. The adrenaline starts to subside and it becomes harder to do the things you've hyped yourself up to cope with. That certainly happened to me.

I ended up sleeping in the RV with Mike. It might have looked like a comfortable and luxurious option compared to the hammocks round the fire – actual beds! Actual bedding! – but in fact it was anything but. What you didn't get to see on TV was that the end of the caravan was open, so the jungle essentially invaded and moved in with us. It felt as though every creature in the rainforest was looking at it as an opportunity to find a nice warm place for the night, much like ourselves, I guess. This meant we were sharing the space with a host of creepy-crawlies and that, along with Mike snoring and me trying to avoid thinking about whatever it was I could feel at the bottom of my sleeping bag, was exhausting. One morning I'd just had enough. I'd been in the Bush Telegraph saying I was having a bit of a wobbly morning then took myself quietly to the RV to pull myself together. I guess the Telegraph people must have told Mike, and he came to find me and make sure I was okay – and that was all I needed for the floodgates to open. But Magic Mike's power soon brought my humour back. I told him I was crying because I'd hit a wall. I was just so tired and I didn't want to sleep with him any more. When I said that he responded, 'How do you think Zara [his wife] feels?' And that was all it took to make me laugh, blow my nose and get myself back out there.

Being in the jungle was an experience I will never forget. I made friends for life and found an inner strength that surprised me – and which I am determined to hold on to for good. To think I almost let my fear of creepy-crawlies talk me out of it... It allowed me to grow in a way that I – and maybe others – had never thought possible. My best moment was coming over the bridge and seeing my son's face. 'You nailed it, Mum,' he said to me, and I will never get bored of that. My boy approved of what I had done, even if he was amazed I ever did it in the first place. He was proud of me and that meant everything.

My time in camp showed me that I might be sixty, but it is never too late to push yourself, to take a risk, to try something new. And that's how I also ended up saying yes to being Mother Superior in the UK touring production of the musical *Sister Act*. It was my first ever stage role, which was a tad daunting, but the stage has always been my first love, so when they asked me if I fancied it, I figured I could either sit there and be terrified, or I could choose to ignore that voice and say 'thanks very much' and get on with it. I'm determined now that if I am interested in something,

I will say 'yes' and not allow the 'what ifs' to creep in. A musical was something new for me. Am I a singer, a dancer? I am not. Am I game for giving anything I fancy a go now? You bloody bet your life I am. (Oh, and I also look pretty good in a wimple.)

## TIPS

- Let go of fear, because fear causes the most suffering.
- Never let being nervous get in the way of doing something new or exciting. As the old saying goes, feel the fear and do it anyway.
- Never think that it's too late to try something new. It isn't!
- Put as much time and effort into building or taking care of your mental health/fitness as you do your physical fitness.
- Find what brings you joy – no matter how big or small.

# 19

## Working Through the Panic

Over the course of our lives we are taught many skills that might help us out in difficult situations. This is all very well in theory, but it doesn't necessarily guarantee that we will be able to put them into practice in an emergency. As a child I might have been able to retrieve a plastic brick from the bottom of a swimming pool while wearing pyjamas, but who knows whether I would be as adept at rescuing a real-life person from the depths, whether in nightwear or not? Likewise, demonstrating an emergency stop in an empty street during your driving test is absolutely not the same as slamming on the brakes when you're doing thirty miles an hour because a small child has just run into your path. You never quite know whether you'll be able to do it for real – until you have to do it for real. When the adrenaline kicks in and the panic takes over.

The work I've done so far – and the Three Principles in particular – has helped me to make so many positive changes to my life. But in extremis would I still be able to put everything I have learned into practice? It turns out the answer is yes – but it took a recent life-threatening emergency for me to find out.

I had a hysterectomy. A relatively straightforward operation that required feet up for a period of recovery before going back to work, socialising, life as it was before. Or so I thought. But I was unlucky. There were a few minor snags, which was one thing, but I got through those okay. But then something else came along out of the blue and it went downhill from there. All at once things took a turn that no one had expected.

Suddenly I was lying on a trolley in the back of an ambulance, blue lights flashing, siren wailing as I was transported from one hospital to another. I became aware that my thinking was going to dark places. I had very low blood pressure and my body was already in fight-or-flight mode. I realised that this was serious and found myself wondering, *Is this how I die?* And it was there, in the back of that ambulance, I heard a bit of my inner wisdom come to the fore, telling me to quiet myself down. I knew that, given what was happening, it was okay to get caught up in it all, it was only human to be scared under those circumstances. But it helped me so much to have that awareness, to be able to listen to that little voice saying, *It's okay, they've got you*. And goodness me, that helped.

And then I was in intensive care. I'd never experienced anything like that before and I was scared, in pain, in shock. I was drugged to the eyeballs with morphine and convinced some poor nurse was trying to do me harm when they were all, in fact, angels. I thought the bed was trying to eat me and there was an endless strange sound playing over and over that felt like it was soundwaves sent by an alien (I eventually discovered it was actually a printer outside my door) and a frog demon sat on my chest blinking at me. Sue being dramatic again? You got it.

Thankfully, I was only in ICU for a very short time – just a few days; I can't imagine what it's like if you're in there longer. When I came out, I was surprised at how wobbly I felt. It affected everything. My voice was different; instead of being strong, it was weak and fluttery. Other people said they could hear the fear and trauma when I spoke, which is not great when you're an actor relying on your voice. For a couple of weeks I just felt overcome, though at the same time I was also aware of the fact that there were people who had been through far worse. But the fear was there. I'd say to my husband, 'Hold my hand, it's happening again.' My hands would tremble, my breathing would be shallow, and I just had to wait for it to ease. I knew it was panic and I knew how panic works, so I recognised it, sat back and let it run its course and tried not to panic about panicking.

That's the thing with panic attacks. Often it's not the event that's the problem, but our thinking around the event. For example, we have an anxious thought, the adrenaline surges, and we get these sensations. Our heart beats faster, our breathing becomes shallower, our hands tremble and we feel like jelly because of the perceived threat. That's normal. That's the body doing its job. But after a while, the body resets itself. It instinctively knows how to look after you.

Here's an example: you might be driving to work. Someone runs out in front of your car. You brake and the adrenaline kicks in and your fight-or-flight response is activated with all the sensations that comes with it. The child is now safely on the pavement and going merrily on their way, but you are still shaken. You might swear – 'What the fuck are you doing?' – and then you will put the car back in gear and drive off. You see a parking space and your attention moves to reversing into that space. You think about putting the handbrake on, remember to lock the door, take the keys and then continue with your day. The system is operating as it should.

But what if we focus on feelings of panic and allow them to eclipse everything else? Instead of rationalising it, we start to panic about the panic. *Oh God, it's here. Oh God, I can't breathe. Oh God, I'm panicking. Oh God, I'm going to die.* I'm pretty sure that no one has died from a panic attack. The worst that will happen is that you might pass out briefly. Why? Because your brilliant, amazing body has done that to stop the cycle and reset the system. How fucking amazing are we?

If you get into the habit of asking yourself, 'Am I anxious?' what you are actually doing is pre-empting the future. So you'll start going, 'Yes, yes, I think I might be anxious. I think I'm feeling anxious,' and the spiral begins. It was Sarie who made me understand how easy it is to innocently talk yourself into a panic attack. *What if I panic? Hang on, is my breathing changing? I think it is. Is my heart beating fast? I think I feel hot. Oh God, I'm dizzy.* And then there you are, in the thick of it. But she also told me about this thing where you can change the habit by bringing it into the present by adding 'right now' to your question. So I might be in the middle of a panic attack, but I ask myself, 'Realistically, am I okay right now?' And the answer would always be yes. I am okay. I'm alive. I'm breathing. It doesn't mean that you don't feel uncomfortable, but we just need to get used to that uncomfortable feeling and in doing so, in getting used to it, you take away its potency.

In the first two weeks after coming out of hospital I kept feeling my adrenaline spike. It wasn't a nice feeling, which is why I wanted my husband to hold my hand. But I acknowledged it and reminded myself that this was all materialising because of something that had happened to me, but that it was now in the past. It was done. I told myself, *It's gone. I'm okay. It will pass.* And as the weeks went by, those episodes became fewer and fewer. The bad stuff was in my head, a hangover from the recent past, but I was in the present and recovering well. Remembering that diminished the power of the feelings that caused me to panic. So can I still see the frog demon or the invasive procedures I went through? Only if I choose to conjure them up. And I choose not to. They don't serve me well. I'm not, of course, diminishing real trauma, but just trying to offer an example of how, in our everyday life, we can give power to these things. Things can and do go wrong for all of us, and accepting that means you can be more realistic and better at appraising situations. It helps you understand that you are able only to change what you're able to change – and so you learn to accept the things you can't.

## TIPS

- Try not to panic about panicking. Understanding what's happening to you physically will help to calm your mind and realise that you will get through it.
- Try to avoid pre-empting what *might* happen and focusing on worst-case scenarios.
- You can bring yourself back to the present by asking yourself how you are *right now*.

# Epilogue

Everything I have been through has played a part in making me me, and my experiences and my studies and discoveries have also helped to shape the woman I am today. But we are so much bigger than the sum of ourselves. I find it fascinating that we become the people we are. We are beautifully flawed; we are truly amazing.

Do we ever really think about how amazing we are? Think about the chances of you being you in terms of being born. According to sources I've read, apparently the chances of us being us are one in 400 trillion. It's down to your mum and dad mating at the exact time they did. One sperm out of millions met one egg out of 300,000. If they'd waited a month longer, you wouldn't be here. It took the exact right sperm and the exact right egg to create you. And we're only getting started – try applying the same process to your four grandparents, your eight great-grandparents, your sixteen great-great-grandparents, all the way down to 3.9 billion years of your ancestral line. If one of those ancestors died or didn't have kids, you would not exist. All of those exact environmental and ecological events had to occur throughout the history of life on Earth to bring you to the here and the now.

We should be celebrating the fact that we are miracles. The odds of us being here, the chances of us even existing are practically zero. This is summed up beautifully by a great Buddhist teaching that says: imagine there is a lifebuoy thrown somewhere into an ocean and there is only one specific turtle in all the oceans swimming underwater. The probability that you will appear and exist is as small as the probability that that turtle will stick its head out of the water into the middle of the lifebuoy in a single attempt. It's pretty incredible when you think about it. *We* are incredible.

And yet here we are, constantly questioning ourselves and wondering whether we are doing life right. The answer is yes! (Unless you are purposely hurting another human being, of course.) Feeling shit, sad, angry, blissful, happy – the entire spectrum of emotion is what it is to be human, but it was only when I realised how this all worked that my life got easier. I still faced the same problems, felt the same joys, disappointments, excitement, pain. I just didn't place so much importance on the content of my thinking. Some days I can be more aware of it than others. Some days I can score a B+, which is brilliant, and other days an F. But the fact is that one thought can change the course of your life. I changed my mind – it's literally that simple.

As for the way I have learned to think about things, I am not an expert, but I am a human whose curiosity led me to study and explore and evolve to find a way to make changes in my own life that have made a hugely positive difference. Here I have brought to the table the wonderful things that other people have shown to me with generosity and kindness (and I have referenced all these wise souls who are just further down the line in their journeys and understanding at the back of this book). Some of these things might be just what you are looking for. Some may work for you, others might offer a jumping-off point for you to look further in a different direction. Any which way, I strongly believe that each one of us has the capacity to find what works for us to bring us closer to feeling innately well. For me, this has been a pretty good place to start:

- Always be curious (it's only through curiosity you can make changes).
- Don't settle for anything for comfort or ease or to be nice.
- You don't need lots of people around you to have a fulfilling life.
- Make your own decisions.
- Always advocate for yourself.
- Learn to be your own support system.
- Set your own boundaries.
- Earn your own money.

Over the last few years I think we have all universally felt out of control, thanks to the pandemic. Humans want security and predictability; we have an inherent desire for order and understanding. The unknown naturally causes us fear and some discomfort, and we don't like it when we cannot influence our environment. I learned that in the jungle. It was exhausting being on high alert, not knowing what was coming next, and also realising that what was coming was likely going to be unpleasant (although probably not as unpleasant as the images I played in my head). That was the ideal time for me to practise what I preach or believe, to try not to dwell on what's next or those 'what if's. Did it work all the time? Absolutely not. As I've said before, I'm human. Sometimes my thoughts run away with me. I do things I regret. I react. But I know that this is usually based on old, learned patterns and behaviours that once served me but no longer do so. What has changed is that I don't beat myself up as much. I see every day as an opportunity to look at things in a different way, to reconsider what I believe to be true. In the very wise words of Scarlett O'Hara in *Gone with the Wind*, 'After all, tomorrow is another day.'

In fact one of the most important takeaways from everything I have been through and all the things I've learned is to consider how often we innocently make life harder for ourselves by misusing the system, as it were. The problem is not that we have bad or sad thoughts, it's what we make of them – i.e. 'I feel like I'm a failure' equates to 'I am a failure'. When thoughts make us feel bad, it is a sign that they are unreliable and untrustworthy – and no amount of thought or rumination is going to help. Let them go in one ear and out the other. Maybe we all need to take ourselves less seriously.

It strikes me that this is an interesting time to be ageing as a woman, when the boundaries between 'old' and 'young' are becoming more blurred than ever before. Gone are the days when you 'had' to look a certain way when you hit sixty. It would be goodbye to the shoulder-length bob and hello shampoo and set (ideally with a purple rinse, of course). Farewell to anything with a hint of style and welcome to fifty shades of beige – anything to enhance that invisibility – and the clothes you can only buy from those ads at the back of the *Radio Times*. But what seemed to be obligatory transition periods where we moved from TopShop to Jane Norman to M&S have vanished, and now we can wear what the hell we like and who cares what anyone else thinks. As generations we are merging, and ultimately that can only be a good thing – even if it takes us a while to get there.

As we look forward to making the most of our middle years – and beyond – we need to focus on finding the things we love, that bring us joy. They don't have to be big things and we don't need to change the world – unless we want to – but no matter how big or small, we should aim for them and pursue them. So whether it's achieving a lifelong ambition or just having time for you, whether it's being the best grandma or taking up a new sport or hobby, it's all about finding the joy in yourself. I love that this can manifest itself in so many different ways, yet it all comes down to the same thing: finding contentment within. All you need to strive for is that feeling of 'I'm all right, I'm okay'. Find what inner peace and happiness looks like for you – and if you're already there, good on you.

We should be proud of who we are. Younger people may choose to see those of us who are in midlife and beyond as rigid and stuck in our ways. The reality is that we have experience and wisdom, we have topped up our skillsets with every challenge we have faced while we raised our families or held down jobs, or cared for sick or elderly parents, and maintained friendships while coping with menopause and whatever life has chosen to throw at us. We have learned to be peacekeepers and negotiators. We make great mentors, team leaders, dispute solvers. We are creative and resourceful and we get things done. We need to remember that and not allow ourselves to be diminished by self-limiting beliefs that will hold us back. (In this I am guilty as charged. I have always believed that I am really shit at maths. But maybe I just had a bad teacher. Maybe the teacher told me I was crap at maths, so I thought it must be true and have allowed myself to hold on to that ever since. Have I tried learning maths in a new way? No. Because the memory of what maths means to me has kept me prisoner. So maybe, after publishing this book, I will do my maths GCSE!)

And yet we still don masks to hide the things we don't want other people to see, to cover all those negative or weak traits that we have innocently come to believe make us unworthy, unlovable and simply not enough. We are surrounded by physical examples of masks everywhere we look: Halloween, Mardi Gras, masks for religious practices, masks to protect against Covid, but all too often we choose to wear self-constructed masks which become the equivalent of a suit of armour; we use them to hide who we are at heart, to hide the vulnerable parts of ourselves so no one can hurt us. We choose to show the world only the faces we choose, which, ultimately, is exhausting. When we allow people to see these masks we create, it feeds into our belief that we are lacking. But if we don't think we are enough, if we don't value ourselves, why would we assume that anyone else is going to?

We need to start being our own best friend. We need to stop hiding. Compassion, love and greater awareness are all we need to let those masks slip. We should never expect everyone to 'get' us or even to like us. The relationship we have with ourselves is the greatest and most important relationship we will ever hope to have in this life.

It is time for us to put down the shackles of our fucked-up thoughts and realise that the keys hanging round our necks have always been within reach. We are unique. We have tried to be everything to everyone and it's so important that we take full advantage of our age and lived experiences to take stock to understand ourselves better, and now give ourselves all that we have given to our children, our parents, our friends, our families, our colleagues.

You are enough. You belong. You are everything.

I see you; your sisters see you. And now you need to make the choice to see it for yourself.

# RESOURCES

As promised at various points in the book, I have put together this list of some of the websites, books and other resources I have found to be useful reading at various times in my own journey. It's not a finite list by any means, but I hope it will at least offer some jumping-off points for you to find out more for yourself.

## BOOKS

*The Missing Link: Reflections on Philosophy and Spirit* by Sydney Banks (the quote on pages 187–8 is taken from this book and used here with the kind permission of Lone Pine Publishing). Note: Syd Banks has also written a number of other very useful books, including *The Enlightened Gardener*.

*The Alcohol Experiment: How to Take Control of Your Drinking and Enjoy Being Sober for Good* by Annie Grace

*This Naked Mind* by Annie Grace

*What the F*ck Are the Three Principles?: And 18 Other Questions Answered from So-Called Wisdom* by Amir Karkouti

*The Complete Guide to the Menopause* by Annice Mukherjee

*The Primal Wound: Understanding the adopted child* by Nancy Newton Verrier

*Never Broken, Nothing Lacking* by Bill Pettit

*Seduced by Consciousness* by Jack Pransky

*Anxiety is a F*#!@? OR IS IT?: Let's Get Started Changing Your Relationship With Anxiety* by Sarie Taylor

On transactional analysis:

*The Games People Play* by Eric Berne

*Scripts People Live* by Claude Steiner (for more than an introductory level)

*The Warm Fuzzy Tale* by Claude Steiner (a children's book, but good for adults too)

*TA Today: A New Introduction to Transactional Analysis* by Ian Stewart and Vann Joines

## WEBSITES

www.youtube.com/c/DickenBettinger

thisnakedmind.com/the-alcohol-experiment/

sydbanks.com/

3pgc.org/ (Three Principles Global Community)

worldwidewellbeing.co.uk (Saric Taylor)

## PODCASTS

*We're Listening*, Rob Cooke

*Psychology Has it Backwards*, Christine Heath and Judy Sedgeman

## VIDEOS

Syd Banks video lecture series, sydbanks.com/videostream/

## POETRY

*Autobiography in Five Short Chapters* by Portia Nelson

# ACKNOWLEDGEMENTS

I am so grateful for the professional support provided during the writing of this book. I had never considered how many people it takes to move from conception to publication, and my thanks go to Bloomsbury Publishing, especially Katy Follain for trusting me, Fabrice Wilmann, Helen Upton, Caroline Bovey, Beth Maher and Rachel Ren. My literary agent Amanda Harris for your unfaltering belief in this project, Elise Middleton at YMU and Cari Rosen for your expertise in shaping this and, in times of writer's block, sustaining me with chicken recipes. Thanks to my husband and partner in crime Brian for tolerating my obsessive attachment to the keyboard and pen. My family, especially Mum and my brother Paul for your love and unwavering support. My half-sister Emma and Kate for your acceptance and generosity. My friends, aka 'the usual suspects', with a shout out to Lisa and Ed, my ride or dies, and a special mention to Sarie Taylor and Jacci Jones as we continue our exploration of what it is to be human – look how far we've come! And finally to my son Elliott, for the joy and lessons you have taught me. I now understand that I cannot stop you leaving every single kitchen cupboard door ajar. I can only change how I choose to respond to it. I choose to laugh.

# A NOTE ON THE TYPE

The text of this book is set in Linotype Sabon, a typeface named after the type founder, Jacques Sabon. It was designed by Jan Tschichold and jointly developed by Linotype, Monotype and Stempel in response to a need for a typeface to be available in identical form for mechanical hot metal composition and hand composition using foundry type.

Tschichold based his design for Sabon roman on a font engraved by Garamond, and Sabon italic on a font by Granjon. It was first used in 1966 and has proved an enduring modern classic.